RETURN TO GOD

The Scottsdale Message

RETURN TO GOD

The Scottsdale Message

Robert Faricy, S. J.
Lucy Rooney, S.N.D.de N.

Queenship Publishing Company
P. O. Box 42028
Santa Barbara, Cal 93140-2028
Phone (800) 647-9882 Fax (805)569-3274

The publisher recognizes and accepts that the final authority regarding the apparitions at Scottsdale, Arizona rests with the Holy See of Rome, to whose judgement we willingly submit.

— The Publisher

About the cover:

Painting donated to St. Maria Goratti in 1991 by the artist M. Musgour depicting our Lady with white Roses.

Cover Design: Janet Schaefer
© 1993 Queenship Publishing Company
All rights Reserved

Library of Congress Catalog Card # 93-84685

Published by:
Queenship Publishing Company
P. O. Box 42028
Santa Barbara, Ca. 93140-2028
Phone (800) 647-9882 Fax (805) 569-3274

Printed in the United States of America

ISBN: 1-882972-09-0

Contents

Note to the Reader

We have written the following pages in order to share with you the events that have been and are now taking place in Scottsdale, Arizona: Jesus and Mary appearing and speaking through a few people but to all of us, calling us to conversion and to acceptance of God's mercy.

In the chapters that follow, we describe the appearances and the words of Jesus and Mary as factual and as authentic, rather than continually refer to them as "reported" or "alleged". The reader will understand that this wording reflects a shared personal belief and opinion pending the outcome of the Church's official investigation.

We want to thank all who have helped us with this book, especially the principal people in it: Stefanie Staab, Steve and Wendy Nelson, Annie Fitch, Jimmy Kupanoff, James Pauley, Susan Evans, Mary Cook, Gianna Talone, and Father Jack Spaulding. We want to thank too Carol Ameche, the staff of Saint Maria Goretti church in Scottsdale, and in a special way Trary Barnes.

This book is dedicated to each of them, in gratitude.

Lucy Rooney, S.N.D. de N.
Robert Faricy, S.J.
London, England, and Melbourne, Australia
February 2, 1993

- I -

What is Going on at Scottsdale

"The main message since our Lady has been coming to me, since I have seen her, is to return to God. And the messages that she gives us are really inspirational and bearing fruit in people's lives. I think revelations and visions and interior voices are all hidden glimpses of the perfection of the faith that lies hidden in each of us. The main fruit for my life is living in this faith. I know it is blind faith for many people; I feel blessed that I see our Lady, but we all share the same faith.

"The fruits — giving, prayer, unity, harmony, restoring dignity, being honest, loving (trying to love anyway, the best way we can) unconditionally, without placing restrictions on people, are showing actually in the lives of not only young adults around here, but also on a national level and an international level. We get letters from people of how the lessons from our Lord and the messages from our Lady have changed their lives dramatically through prayer.

"It takes time, I know in my own life; and it can be frustrating so many times when you would like to snap your fingers and just be the perfect person! What we are all seeing is that God respects our humanity so much that He doesn't force anything on us. With your free will He gives you that choice, and He graces you with wisdom and discernment. So a lot of the struggle starts because we used to be one way, and then we know the love of our Lord. And as we start to change there is always conflict with the old way.

"And then you start gradually, very slowly — it is a slow process — of being independent enough in your free will to love God so much that you make a <u>choice</u> to walk away from the old way, to struggle toward the good way. And then you see even more good fruits. You gain in your self respect, your self identity and love of yourself. So fruits are definitely there. And that is all part of the message and part of returning to God, that He gives us that option, that free will to turn back to Him." (<u>Gianna Talone to Lucy Rooney SND de N, October 2, 1992</u>)

Scottsdale had never come to our attention until the summer of 1990 when we met Annie in Los Angeles. Annie told us that the blessed Virgin Mary was appearing daily in the parish of Saint Maria Goretti, Scottsdale, Arizona. Annie said she was one of nine young people who, with the pastor, were caught up in the events there; they were hearing the voice of our Lady or of our Lord, and in some cases seeing Jesus and Mary.

Having listened to Annie's story, we decided to go to Scottsdale to investigate. And we have returned there many times since. As all Catholics may, having weighed all the evidence and, in our case, having met everyone concerned, we believed. When the Church finally makes a judgment, we will follow that decision. Meanwhile, the important thing is the message for the world which is coming from Jesus and from His Mother. If God and His Mother are coming back to earth, to America, to speak to us today, then we want to take that seriously.

The setting is Scottsdale, Arizona, just northeast of Phoenix in the Valley of the Sun. In the 1920's Scottsdale was described as a place of "thirty-odd tents and half a dozen adobe houses". In seventy years it has grown to be a town of 130,000 people, a major metropolitan area of Phoenix. It is ringed by pinkish sandstone mountains sharply serrated against the blue sky. Beyond is desert. The Valley of the Sun is watered by the Colorado and Salt rivers. Fifty thousand native Americans, from seventeen tribes, live in the twenty-three reservations of Arizona. The Salt River Reservation is just east of Scottsdale. About half of the Arizona population is Catholic, many Hispanic Americans. Scottsdale itself appears affluent. The mild, dry winters are an attraction to retired people, and "the most western town in the west" has a growing tourist industry. Paradise Valley, part of the parish of Saint Maria Goretti, was a desert fifty years ago. Recently a visitor described it as "a millionaires' ghetto".

The nine young adults concerned in the Scottsdale events had each, in the late summer of 1988, gone separately to Father Jack Spaulding, pastor of Saint Maria Goretti parish, several to say, "Father Jack, I must be going crazy. This voice is speaking to me." In no way a group, most did not know each other, or had just seen each other around. They ranged, then, in age from nineteen to thirty one: six young women — Annie, Gianna, Mary, Stefanie, Susan and Wendy; and three young men — James, Jimmy and Steve.

Father Jack Spaulding the pastor, Vicar Forane of the Phoenix diocese and at one time Chancellor, had been told by Gianna Talone of a vision in which she had seen the nine in the presence of our Lady. She and six others were kneeling. Two were standing, one of whom she recognized as Stefanie. The other she eventually knew to be Annie. Father Jack, prepared for their coming, told each not to speak to anyone about their experience. They were therefore quite uninfluenced until he called them together.

With Gianna Talone, at that time thirty years old and a Doctor of Pharmacology, events had begun in September, 1987, with what she at first thought was a dream of our Lady standing beside her bed and praying silently over her. Only when the "dream" was repeated on three consecutive nights did she know it was a reality. The following year, June, 1988, she went with her mother and a group from the parish, to Medjugorje, Yugoslavia, where the Mother of God has been appearing for over a decade. There our Lady spoke to Gianna for the first time. Father Jack was neither pleased nor convinced when she told him. She too wanted to deny the experience, worried that her mental balance must be upset. She decided to go to the house of Vicka, one of the visionaries at Medjugorje. It was almost impossible to approach Vicka because of the crowds. So Gianna thought she would just walk by and forget the whole affair. But as she approached the house, the crowd parted, and there was a clear path bringing her face to face with Vicka. Without any enquiry, Vicka asked Gianna to return the next day with an interpreter. At that meeting Vicka confirmed that the voice was that of our Lady, and that Gianna should expect further messages upon her return to Scottsdale.

Since then both Jesus and Mary have appeared to Gianna and have spoken with her frequently. The blessed Mother first appeared to Gianna at home, on December 19, 1989. She began appearing in the church of Saint Maria Goretti, on December 28, 1989, to Gianna and to Annie, during the rosary at the parish Thursday evening prayer group.

Our Lady's coming, they both say, is preceded by a brilliant light. She seems to come out of the statue of Our Lady of Guadalupe which is to the left of the altar, but then does not resemble it. They describe her as young, dark haired, and so beautiful as to be beyond description. She continues to appear daily to Gianna, except on Fridays when she has asked her to make the sacrifice of not seeing her.

Gianna once remarked to us that she could not wish for anyone to see Jesus or our Lady because of the suffering that ensues. Both Annie and Gianna were obviously in ecstasy when we have observed them during an apparition, yet despite this rapture, the experience has led them into a "communion in the sufferings of Christ" (Philippians 3:10). Gianna's husband left her during this time, seeking a divorce. The marriage has been annulled by the Church. This was the beginning of many sufferings. Spiritual darkness is, at some time, inevitable for all of us. Often it coincides with difficulties in our lives, as when Gianna lost her job just after losing the husband she loved. At the same time she has come to know "the love of Christ which surpasses knowledge". (Ephesians 3:19) In all this, what is God saying to us? Here is one of the messages:

Message to the Thursday Prayer Group at Saint Maria Goretti Church, given by Our Lady through Gianna, 23 January, 1992

My dear children, I come to ask you to pray and to love.

I come because my Son is Love, and He loves you all, his beloved children. My dear little ones, begin first to love your family. Be love to one another.

Please beware that Satan is trying to cause division and disrupt unity not only in the family but in the world. Form together in love as a strong unit and you will have the shield to protect you against his attempts.

I love you my little ones, and bless you in the name of my Son. Thank you for responding to my call.

For Annie Ross Fitch the beginning was on 31 March 1989 during the ceremony of dedication of the statue of Our Lady of Guadalupe in Saint Maria Goretti church. During the dedication of the statue that evening, Annie heard a woman's voice, outside herself, saying, "My child, you must make a decision. You must decide to give your life to me, or not. But you must make the decision now. There is no more time." Annie says, "I walked up to the statue as everyone else did, with my flowers, to place them at her feet. I kissed her feet and I gave her my heart ... I told her that she could have all of me, that I would make that decision. I walked away sobbing."

When Annie let herself into her apartment that night, the voice spoke to her again: "My child, I wish for you to write." She was astounded, scared, though at the same time reassured by the gentle melodic tone of the voice and by the feelings of peace, joy and serenity that it inspired in her. But she searched the house thinking that friends might be playing a joke. She was alone, and the voice was gently repeating, "My child, I want you to write." After several false starts in finding paper, a pen that would write, a pencil that would not break, she took down the message dictated by the voice. It was clearly our Lady speaking. Annie says "I was filled with incredible peace and so filled with love! I had so much anger, and so much hatred had built up inside of me - because of the things I had been through in my life - suddenly all of those things were gone". Since then Annie has been in constant communication with the blessed Mother. Jesus too speaks to her.

In speaking to Annie, Jesus and Mary have been loving but firm in helping her to change her life. During Lent, 1991, they worked with her daily on different habits: "A tough time", says Annie. Earlier our Lady had corrected her for taking the writing of the messages 'lightly'. Mary said, "In your joy and in your enthusiasm you are harming yourself and my other chosen ones. Silence, my dear one, is crucial! Silence is a gift, a grace. It is difficult and sometimes painful."

Special tasks that have been given to Annie are to pray for an end to abortion and to intercede for priests and religious.

Annie has been shown the admonishments and chastise-ments that await the world. She says she shuddered. At the same time both Jesus and Mary have told her that Saint Maria Goretti church will be the center of God's love and mercy for all.

Jesus has appeared to Annie, but she has more often seen Him in visions. Our Lady, having appeared to her regularly beginning December 28, 1989, told Annie on October 18, 1990, that this was to be her last regular apparition. She would appear to her on her birthday and at times of difficulty. Annie says, "She was more beautiful, more radiant than I had ever seen her. She thanked me, (thanking me!) for giving my life to her ... I cried when she left. I wasn't crying because she was gone, but because I hadn't done enough. Even if I were to give every moment for the rest of my life for her, it would never be enough."

To be champion steer wrestler and calf roper had long been the ambition of twenty-six year old Steve Nelson. He was well on the way to achieving it when a voice began speaking to him. Steve, blond, five feet nine, was no fervent Catholic: "I was going to church to keep mom and dad happy, but ... I wasn't living the kind of life I should have been living." He was living away from home to be near the rodeo, but began coming back to the parish "Next thing I know, I couldn't get enough of it. I started getting in-volved." Steve moved back, started praying and going to daily Mass. Jesus and Mary speak to him in his heart. At first he panicked, thinking he would have to be a priest, whereas marriage was what attracted him. He weighed up the difficulties of being a priest until his mom one day dryly remarked, "What's marriage? Chopped liver?" He put his ambitions and everything else in his life "on hold" until he could see where he was being led.

What Steve values most is being who he is: "Our Lord and our Lady can't want me to be anything more than what I am. They called me as Steve Nelson the way Steve Nelson was, because they loved who I am." Steve sums up what all the nine young people say when he points out that he is just a normal person with the same struggles as everyone else. "I think it is my sinfulness that makes me more real in helping people. I still have just as many stumbling stones as the next person. ... The one thing our Lady has shown me is this: 'Steve, I need you to be you, and to show people that even though you have hard times, even though things go up and down, if you have hope and trust, you can still carry around joy and peace'."

Susan Evans would agree. "I told our Lord the other day, 'You know, a righteous person can't really lead a person back to You. It is a sinner who leads a sinner back to You because a sinner has understanding'." Susan has learned this from what she regards as her failures. Dark haired, vivacious Susan, born in January, 1958, experienced the intervention of the Lord before the events at Scottsdale began. She was with her family at a wedding reception when a voice startled her: "Would you give up your family for me?" Susan says, "We were sitting at a round table in the garden. I looked at each one of them, and I finally answered, "Yes Lord, because I love You more." When we quoted this in our first book on Scottsdale, Susan was horrified, thinking that her family would conclude that she did not love them. In fact, it was just one example of what the Lord is asking of all caught up in these events, and of all of us, - that we love Him more than ourselves, more than all things, more than all others, even our specially loved ones, while at the same time loving them with Him, more truly than we ever could alone.

The voice led Susan on, asking her if she would suffer for Him, and then on to show her various outwardly unattractive people (for whom of course He had suffered) asking if she too would suffer for them. Susan knows that her 'yes' was not her own offering, but a grace given to her.

At that time Susan had no real devotion to Mary, afraid rather of Mary's perfection. But she began praying to our Lady, begging her to bring her back to the Lord, back to the Church. "And the change!" says Susan. "Within five or six weeks I was back in church. I showed up at Saint Maria Goretti ... My mom was there. She said 'What are you here for?' I started going to Mass every day, and I started to stay on after Mass for a couple of hours to pray. ... I was so drawn to the Eucharist. I cried receiving the Eucharist, because it is such a gift, and because our Lord had brought me away from a sinful life to a better life."

Our Lord's question about suffering was a serious one. Physical illnesses overtook Susan, as well as spiritual trials. Our Lord had warned her to expect a struggle. She had replied, "OK, I'm going to make it a good one." The struggle concerned chastisements which even from childhood she had known about. They had not frightened her then, but now she was agonizing in extreme fear for those who do not believe, or who, believing, do not return to God. Susan struggled. "I started real good for two and a half months. Then finally I got mad at God ... I let it out. You can't hide anything from Him anyway. He just filled me with so much peace. It really gives the devil nothing to work with once you have let it out to God."

Both Jesus and Mary have spoken audibly to Susan, but not often. She talks with them all day in an interior, normal, way. In November, 1987, our Lady told Susan that she wanted a prayer group of young adults. This now meets on Friday evenings.

Our Lady has given to each of the nine young men and women a personal symbol to live out; Susan's is charity. She says that to her charity means, "Giving of yourself. It is a giving of the gifts you have received: love, faith, hope, joy. It is a giving of these gifts to others. At one time I was afraid of this symbol, because charity is also a giving of yourself to our Lord. It got a little scary there for a while because He was asking me to suffer."

Events at Scottsdale have not surprised Susan. Because of something she knew, she has been expecting our Lady's coming since she was a child.

In her vision of the group of nine, Gianna saw Jimmy Kupanoff walk away, and James Pauley come in. Then Jimmy returned. This has been borne out in actuality. Jimmy had begun to pray before becoming involved in the Scottsdale events. He had gone with his family to Medjugorje, and there had a strong realization of Jesus as Lord of all things. It woke him up to the 'miracles' of everyday. When his family moved back from Scottsdale to Ohio, Jimmy stayed on, living for a while in the rectory with Father Jack and his assistant pastor. Then his parents, his three sisters and two younger brothers returned to Scottsdale. Our Lady has spoken to Jimmy a few times in clear interior words, but usually it is a burning in his heart. Father Jack says that Jimmy fought against all this for a long time, but finally said "Yes". Meanwhile he continues to study at Arizona State University, working part time. Jimmy's symbol is compassion.

James Pauley, six foot two, is the youngest of the nine, born in November, 1971. He does not see our Lady nor hear her, but was told by Father Jack Spaulding in 1988 that Gianna had seen him as part of the group of nine. At first, James said, he was excited at the thought of seeing our Lady, because she has told Gianna that they will each see her when they are ready. "It took me a while to cool and be disciplined," James said, "because our Lord is not in the past or the future, but here now." James prays and is at daily Mass whenever possible. His work is as full-time Youth Minister and Director of the Teen Program in the parish. He also works in the three-year program of preparation of candidates for the Sacrament of Confirmation.

In 1991 and 1992 James made speaking tours of England with Father Jack. There he made contact with groups of young people whose lives are formed by their desire to respond to the messages which our Lady has given to the world at Medjugorje. These young adults and the members of the young adults' prayer group at Scottsdale are working out for themselves the import of the unprecedented world-wide apparitions of the blessed Virgin in our times.

We first met Mary Cook at the "Good Egg" restaurant in Scottsdale. Mary had given up a job which she loved, because as she said, "My job was the center of my life. Now I know that Jesus has to be the center of my life." Then she found a work close to her heart. She works with pre-school children, laying, with her colleagues and the parents, a Christian foundation in the children's lives. Obviously gifted for such work, in 1992 Mary set up a parish based pre-school at Saint Maria Goretti.

Father Jack Spaulding has described how Mary came to be involved as one of the nine. "Gianna and Stefanie came to me to say that our Lady would ask Mary Cook. I had known Mary briefly before she moved back to Wisconsin to join her family. Gianna knew her slightly, Stefanie better. Both said Mary had said 'no' but our Lady would ask her again. If she said 'yes', she would be back in Scottsdale again. The very next week when I looked at my appointment book, there was her name! When we met, she had the same look on her face as Gianna and Stefanie had, and she said the same thing, 'I think I am going crazy ... a voice inviting me to come back here and talk to you. I said 'no', and then I said 'yes'.'"

Mary first saw our Lady during the Irvine Medjugorje Conference in 1991. Before that she had seen a dazzling purple glow around the statue in Saint Maria Goretti church, and on one occasion heard clearly the message which is given by the blessed Virgin to Gianna each Thursday for the parish.

Jesus and his Mother converse with Mary. "If I talk to Him, He just talks right to me." she says, and "Our Lady just talks to me." Mary's symbol is hope.

Message from Our Lady to the Young Adults' Prayer Group, given through Mary Cook, 17 January 1992

My dear ones, it is I, your Mother. I am here tonight because my Son allows me to come to you, and because I love you so much! I thank you for being so devoted, so dedicated to my Son. My dear ones, tonight I ask you to make a commitment to prayer. It is very crucial to my plan that you commit yourselves to prayer to my Son. Ask for my intercession and I will help you. I am always reaching my hand out to help you, my little ones. Please take hold. I will lead you to my Son.

Pray with your hearts. Pray with your hearts, little ones, and you will find the answers to my Son's will for you. Pray honestly to Him. There is no need to hide anything. He knows all.

"Will you give me everything?" That was the question that startled Wendy Nelson. Wendy, Steve's sister, younger by three years, grew up with him on ranches in South Dakota and Nebraska. For some time while living in Scottsdale, she had been working with the Sisters of Mother Teresa of Calcutta in Phoenix. For a while she lived with them, sharing their life and learning to pray. At home in Scottsdale she went daily to Mass and often talked with Father Jack Spaulding. Now, hearing a voice and realizing that it was Jesus speaking, she went to see Father Jack. She explains that she did not know that "Gianna had already been to see Him, and Stefanie, and a couple of the others. Father Jack said to just keep it real quiet, to come often and we would pray about it. Then, every now and then I'd be praying, and they (Jesus and Mary) would just say something. Maybe something about Jesus's agony and His passion. Then Father Jack called us all together and said, 'Look, you are all having these things happen.' That is how I got involved in it."

One Thursday Wendy was at the parish prayer group in Saint Maria Goretti. Just after the rosary she saw a bright light around our Lady's statue. "It got so bright that it was just hurting my eyes; so I closed my eyes. Our Lady said, 'Child, look at me' and I could not. I just couldn't look. And then she said, 'Child, look at me with the innocence and purity of a child.' Then she just came out of the statue. She is beautiful! No, we didn't talk; she was just there. It's the kind of thing you don't forget; it's always in the heart. And it's a funny thing when I talk about it, I can just feel it! Oh the love that comes from her! It's just incredible! I'd never experienced love in that way."

Jesus and Mary continue to speak to Wendy. "They come like a friend" she says. Sometimes they speak daily; at other times she can go a week without hearing anything. She says they teach her faith and trust. Perhaps these are the components of her symbol which is strength.

Jazz enthusiast, skier, target shooter, Stefanie Staab has as her symbol joy. She says, "Since our Lady came, she turned my life around - she did a lot for me ... I've softened up a lot; I'm more like who I think God created me to be."

Stefanie was the second of the nine to come to Father Jack. He says, "Stefanie is a brilliant young woman. She works with accounting firms. ... She didn't go to church very much but started coming to our prayer group. I had seen her around. She came in one day and said exactly the same as Gianna did, "I think I am going crazy Father. I am hearing a voice." Stefanie had received a number of messages. As she handed one of them to Father Jack, she said, "This voice said this; I didn't." Father Jack comments: "After I read it, I knew she didn't say it. She couldn't know what it was. It was about conversion of heart, and it was one of the most beautiful theological and pastoral treatises that I have ever read on what converting your heart means. ... As far as religion goes, Stefanie hadn't a clue, nor had she any theological background."

Stefanie gave up a prestigious job until she found what she thought our Lord wanted her to do with her life. Now she works, as do the others, for the usefulness of the work and to pay her bills, rather than for prestige and wealth.

During the meeting of the young adults' prayer group on Friday evenings, our Lady and sometimes Jesus speak through

Stefanie, giving a message to the group, usually for their own lives. Jesus often speaks through Gianna, our Lady through Mary Cook and occasionally through Annie. Anyone from eighteen to thirty-five may attend the group. The only adults are Father Jack Spaulding and Carol Ameche, a lady of the parish who records and types the messages. If neither are present, no messages are given.

Before the young adults' prayer group began, up to fifteen friends met each Saturday to pray together. They were called together by a locution given to Stefanie. She was told whom to invite; but in asking each one, she merely said, "We have a prayer meeting. Would you like to come?" Perhaps because the group was small and close-knit, the messages they received were often personal or about their life together as a group. Stefanie says that the messages and lessons taught them many things, and personal things - ways to change. She says the group members were of differing backgrounds, leading different lives. They challenged each other and matured.

Some of them felt a call to celibacy; but as none of the group were at that time married, this teaching from Jesus, received by Stefanie, was applicable to all:

> My dear one, thank you, please open your notebook. - My dear one, your greatest fear of being alone has been answered by me with grace. It is my mercy and love that has brought your sisters to the point of understanding, and it is time to be samples. Can you accept celibate love? This is the question I wish to be posed to all my couples of men and women who have been joined together as samples.

My dear ones, you know not the deception Satan can cast upon you when you allow your lower faculties to rule you and to be your refuge. It is true that the love I call all of you to is one of purity and self-denial. Deny yourselves first for me and then for one another. I wish it so.

Each of you girls in this house is to be a sample of purity, chastity and innocence. I ask you, "Can you deny your flamboyant ways; desire to obtain this attention, and allow my Mother's grace to enter you?" You shall shine, my dear ones, shine with purity and grace. Clothe yourselves in chastity, chaste garments, chaste actions and chaste attitudes towards others, especially the men I have brought.

Men, my sons, are you willing to give up your egotistic actions and attitudes? Will you accept these women as symbols of my Mother's purity, and treat them as you would my own dear Mother? - Would you seek to possess her? Would you lust after her, the one full of grace? My dear sons, you would not. I tell you, no matter how poor in spirit one was, my Mother's grace dazzled their heart and left them with peace.

I wish to sanctify each of these girls, shearing away from them the hardness of the world. Can you accept them for the gems they shall become, and guard them carefully with your virtues? Your virtues - I tell you, they shall multiply. Man was created along with woman to be his helpmate. Do you think this statement is of the physical? It is a statement of the spiritual. Through these women much grace shall flow, and it shall flow often unto you. Can you love them for this and not for the physical?

My dear sons, do you think I ask much of you? I, if you will say 'yes', shall sanctify your hearts. There are many ways to accomplish this but what I offer to you now is the love of a pure and chaste relation between a man and a woman. Be one another's spiritual helpmate.

Do not, I caution you, attach your own meaning to my divine words. Focus on my Mother and ask for the sanctification of your souls through her presence and my grace which I give to her, and leave all else to me. You shall understand more fully as it is time and you are made ready. Pray my children for the grace to say 'yes' to my call.

Stefanie adds that she asked Jesus what he wanted her to do with this message. He replied that each girl had been sent someone, and it was up to them to accept them. It was up to each man to accept the call, and up to Father Jack to school the group. (July 15, 1989)

Message from Our Lady to the Young Adults' Prayer Group, given through Stefanie, 23 January 1992

My dear children, it is I your Mother who comes to you again to thank you for your joy; to thank you for your faithfulness.

My dear children, know that I need your prayers, your love, your devotion. I need it all so that many graces may be shed upon all those who are in need. There are so many, my dear ones, who are so gravely in need of your love, your compassion, your prayers and your devotion to this cause of mercy.

I beg you my dear ones, renew your devotion: your devotion to prayer, to sacrifice, to conversion. My dear ones, ask the Lord to multiply the fruits of His grace in your lives, in your hearts, in your minds, in your speech, in your habits, in all your capacities so that God's grace may be shed through each one of you out to the world that surrounds you.

I pray, my dear ones, with heartfelt joy and the deepest desire for you to become my perfect instruments that I may bundle you to my heart.

How has the pastor, Father Jack Spaulding, reacted to these events in his parish? At first, with dismay and impatience. When Gianna first told him during the pilgrimage to Medjugorje that a voice was speaking to her, he was irritated. People on pilgrimage can be carried away. Apparitions inevitably are followed by "copy cat" claims.

Dismayed as Father Jack Spaulding was as these events began in his parish, he is too much a man of God to go against what the Lord might be doing. Prudently, he used all the criteria the Church provides for determining, as far as may be possible, the authenticity of the experiences described by the nine. Locutions and apparitions can never be proved, not even those at Lourdes and Fatima. The most the Church can say is that the alleged events are supernatural in origin, or that conversely, they are not of supernatural origin. A small commission appointed by Phoenix Bishop Thomas O'Brien, did not make either of these statements. The commission said in October, 1989, that it could find no evidence that events were not supernatural, nor could they find evidence to prove they were of supernatural origin. The parish activities and the prayer groups could continue as usual.

In believing the nine young people, Father Jack opened himself to ridicule. Even more so when in August, 1988, our Lady spoke to him during a visit to Medjugorje. Some of his fellow priests and some lay people thought him crazy when in November of the same year Jesus and our Lady began speaking through him during his homilies at the Thursday evening prayer group Mass. Like the others involved, Father Jack has suffered many hurts and needs repeatedly to forgive. Though he and Father Dale Fushek continue to produce films for Catholic Life Productions, their programs have been banned from the Catholic station, Eternal Word Television Network, and this without his having been informed personally. A normally volatile man, Father Jack has responded to all the disbelief with serene faith. Who are we to decide what God can or may do? Father Jack's inherent need to be in control of any situation has been superseded by a vigilant faith, peace and trust.

He emphasizes that he is free to say 'no', as are the nine young people. "God and our Lady never, never interfere with our free will, ever. They always invite. Every now and then they ask us, 'Do you want to continue to say 'yes'? If you want to say 'no', we will not love you any less'."

Father Jack sees the Scottsdale events as a call to conversion. "I have come to realize", he says, "that there are two conversions. The first is conversion of life - we have some control over that as it continues on: changing behavior, changing attitudes. Real conversion, conversion of heart - over that we have no control except to say 'yes' to the Lord. The Lord is the one who does that in His time and in His way. Most of the time it is not how we would do it!"

Message given by Our Lord through Father Jack Spaulding at the Friday night Young Adult Prayer Group, 31 January 1992

My dear children, I love you with all my Being. I do give you my comfort, my grace, this night. Know that I am with you. And my heart this night is full of gratitude for your devotion.

Your struggles will cease, my dear ones, the closer you come to me as I am present to you in my most blessed Sacrament. I am here always! Present to me this night any fear you have. Exchange that fear for my joy.

I bless your hearts. Be strong in my peace.

- II -
The Present Situation

Extract from a Message from Our Lady to the Parish Prayer Group, given through Gianna, May 7, 1992

My dear little ones, I come because my Son's love is upon you. Please unite and live in harmony. Be loving and kind. Be compassionate. ... Pray, my dear ones, pray for peace, and <u>forgive</u> one another. ... Thank you for responding to my Son. Come now into His most sacred Heart.

Jesus and Mary have said that the parish of Saint Maria Goretti, Scottsdale, is to be a special place of divine Love and Mercy. There, they are calling us to return to God, to come quickly, to come as we are, to come now. This is the only hope for us individually, and the only hope for our world. If we are each enfolded in the divine Love which is God — Father, Son and Spirit; if we are each enveloped in the divine Mercy which is freely offered, then world peace follows, because to breathe in Love and Mercy for ourselves is to breathe out compassion, forgiveness to others. Harmony and peace follow.

Our Lady has indicated this in her repeated call for the sacrament of Reconciliation to be more available at the church.

On March 5, 1992 she said,

> My dear children, I come to ask you for reconciliation. I, your Mother, see so many broken hearts. Please be open to begin more time for confessions here at this parish for all my children coming. ... It is necessary, here at my Son's center of His divine mercy, so that He can free you and heal you. ... Pray, and prepare for your new beginning through confession.

And again, on April 23, 1992:

> ... Reconcile, my children. I have asked three times now from my Son, for the sacrament of Reconciliation to take place here at His Center of Mercy ...

And Jesus himself reiterated this, speaking through Father Jack, on July 2, 1992:

> My dear ones, as you come here this night to pray, so many ask for healing. I tell you, my dear ones, I wish to heal all of you, but what each of you needs healing of most, you very seldom ask for healing. That area, my dear ones, is the area of your sin. Your sin destroys you; your sin paralyses you; your sin is the cancer of your soul. My dear ones, I ask you and invite you now to give to me your sin so that I may heal you truly. I love you. I have died for you. My Father has raised me up for you ... Do not be discouraged, my dear ones, by your sin. Offer your sin to me. I will heal you. I love you and bless you this night with my peace, my forgiveness, and with my mercy.

More and more people come to the Thursday evening rosary and Mass. Frequently the church cannot accommodate all who arrive. Jesus and Mary continue to speak through Father Jack, though not every Thursday. He longs to respond to our Lady's request for the sacrament of Reconciliation to be more available, but so far there are just two priests, Father Jack and his associate pastor, Father John Coleman, though they are now supported by the diocesan Director of Vocations, Father Harold Graaf, who has moved in with Father Jack.

At first, the intervention of our Lord and of our Lady was hardly known even to some of the parishioners. This was largely because Father Jack and the nine young men and women were meticulous in obeying the local bishop, Bishop Thomas O'Brien who allowed the prayer groups and other parish activities to continue, but forbad direct preaching of the events taking place. But after the publication of Our Lady Comes to Scottsdale: Is It Authentic? (the book that we wrote in 1991 and which was published in faith by Bill and Fran Reck of the Riehle Foundation, Ohio), people all over the United States began to be aware that America was honored by these apparitions. Then the ABC Channel Three Television of Phoenix asked Father Jack for permission to make a documentary. In accordance with obedience to the bishop he refused, but the TV station approached the bishop directly. Bishop O'Brien gave the permission, and the documentary was made in May, 1992. Father Jack, Mary, Susan, Steve and Gianna were filmed praying the rosary, during which our Lady appeared to Gianna. The result was intense local interest - and incidentally ridicule from some, especially, and lamentably, some Catholics, working with those who were interviewed. Gianna had to leave her position at Saint Joseph's Hospital shortly afterwards.

Bishop O'Brien commented publicly on the events at Saint Maria Goretti Parish for the first time since his commission's report in an excellent and balanced article printed in the diocesan newspaper, The Catholic Sun of June 4, 1992. Bishop O'Brien writes:

> Much publicity has been given to Fr. Jack Spaulding, pastor of St. Maria Goretti Parish in Scottsdale, and individuals who are claiming to be receiving messages and apparitions from Jesus our Lord and the Blessed Mother. I thought it might be helpful if I shared some observations.
>
> These alleged messages, which have now been printed in books, generally occur on Thursday evenings during prayer services attended by several hundred people. I have never attended these services, and I'm told that many parishioners were unaware of these alleged occurrences until the recent publicity.
>
> I learned of these events in 1989 and established a small commission to inquire into the nature of them. Subsequently, they reported their findings to me, and I accepted them and published them in early 1990.
>
> THE COMMISSION CONCLUDED at the time that "the events seem to us to be explained as human experiences and by ordinary human dynamics. We are therefore constrained to conclude they are within the order of nature and are not miraculous. The messages (locutions) are explainable within the range of ordinary human experience, but obviously

we cannot know for certain whether or not the locutions or visions are miraculous in the true sense of the word." The commission states also "the commitment to the Lord and the depth of faith in all the individuals involved are beyond question."

About the same time I established another commission to investigate the alleged occurrences surrounding Estela Ruiz, a woman in Phoenix, who was also claiming to be the recipient of messages and visions. That commission reported essentially the same thing.

My position still stands as does the provisional approval I gave to the devotional prayer meetings surrounding the claims. I have no reason or evidence to make further judgment about the origin or authenticity of these events.

IN MY LIMITED discussions with Fr. Spaulding and the others involved, it is very clear that they honestly and sincerely believe they are receiving messages from Jesus and the Blessed Virgin Mary. The messages, in the form of teachings or lessons, speak to us of God's love and call us to be people of faith, prayer, peace and penance.

It's obviously true that God can choose any way or means to reveal Himself. But, our Catholic doctrine holds that He has revealed Himself primarily through Scriptures, the inspired word of God and through the tradition of the Church. There will be no new revelation about God and His plan of salvation for His people.

The role of Mary, and devotion to her, springs from her position in sacred Scripture. As mother of Jesus Christ, she is part of the mystery of faith. This role belongs to public revelation — it is integrated into the deposit of faith carried through the centuries.

Private revelations/apparitions have added greatly to the devotion of the people of God. They are a part of the rich heritage of the Catholic people.

SINCE THESE EXTRAORDINARY phenomena tend to be sensationalized, we need to keep them in perspective. Even when they are authentically supernatural, they are really only support systems; they add nothing new. According to St. Thomas Aquinas, divine interventions of this kind are reminders of what we already know. These messages are not the word of God, and they are not infallible.

As Catholics, our lives are to be guided by God's Word and the Sacraments, especially the Eucharist. You are certainly free to believe in these private revelations/apparitions if you wish. If you choose to do so, however, don't fail to see the forest for the trees. The trees are the extraordinary phenomenon. The forest is the living Christ, dwelling in the community and speaking to us through the public ministry of the Church.

Distinguish between the apparitions/messages and faith itself. Visions and messages are outside the vesture of faith. God and our Lady may use them to teach us in our faith. But faith and faith alone is the point of contact. The important thing is God's presence in faith. The visions and the words are just vehicles and the instrument of the Divine Presence. This presence is the same Presence and the same work of faith as in the rest of our daily lives.

WE WALK BY FAITH and not by sight. Faith is a much more secure guide than private revelations; messages only call our attention to the teaching or faith from which we take directions.

Let us live in the wonderful, spacious world of God, Christ, the Church, the Bible, the Eucharist and the community we are called to serve.

Admittedly, private revelations have immense appeal, but they cannot take us out of the human condition. The value of these phenomena is to get us started, to put us on track as disciples of Jesus and children of Mary. This means we move as soon as we can into the walk of faith.

Bishop O'Brien goes to the heart of the Scottsdale message in his concluding sentence: "The value of these phenomena is to put us back on track as disciples of Jesus and children of Mary. This means we move as soon as we can into the walk of faith."

Our walk of faith is <u>living a full life in Christ</u>. The multiplication of apparitions around the world, so unprecedented, even if only some are authentic, indicates an urgency, almost a desperation on the part of our Lord and Mary our Mother, to wake us up to a renewal of life in Christ before it is too late. We cannot afford not to respond.

Response to the intervention of Jesus and of our Lady has profoundly altered the lives of each of the nine: from James, the youngest, to Wendy, Jimmy, Steve, Mary, Annie, Stefanie, Susan and Gianna.

James' life may not have changed outwardly. He continues as full-time Youth Minister at Saint Maria Goretti Parish, working also with teenagers and having responsibility for Confirmation preparation. James' growth is both spiritual and in character. Aged twenty-one in 1992, he is gentle and unselfconsciously assured, as was evident in the talks he gave throughout the British Isles in two successive years. Being unable, in obedience to the bishop, to speak of events at Scottsdale, James' talks were a witness to the call and the enabling grace that the Lord has for young people in the Church, of the joy and fullness of life offered, rather than the irritating yoke which many young people identify with 'religion'. One of James' joys is to take his youth groups to work at the two missions in Mexico adopted by the parish. Meanwhile, he follows a path of faith, sure of his call, but as yet without seeing or hearing.

Wendy whose twenty-third birthday was August 15, 1992, was asked by the Phoenix city council to work on one of their projects for the poor. This was a Home Shelter for Teens At Risk. Her decision was to accept; but, if the city's sex education program for teen-agers included the offer of condoms, she would resign.

Jimmy now twenty-four, continues part-time studies while he works full time in the parish, especially in the music ministry. One of his specialities is filming for television. With James he leads the youth and Confirmation groups to the Mexican mission at Wymuss. Like the others, his spiritual path is often painful and a struggle, but he has been described as "an inspiration to others".

Steve, three years older than his sister Wendy, having put his life 'on hold' until he understood the Lord's calling, was married in June 1992 to Susan Rehab. In this new phase of his life he turned to Saint Joseph, asking to be taught how to be a man, a husband and a worker. A mistake, says Steve, laughing! He has so much work he cannot fit it all into his days. He is an accomplished carpenter and house painter.

Mary, now aged twenty-nine, continues to see our Lady, but interiorly, not coming from the statue as with Gianna and Annie, though she does see our Lady in her statue glow and smile. Her locutions from the blessed Mother are interior too, but verbal - a voice clearly heard. Her messages are usually personal ones; but in the absence of Gianna during the summer of 1992, Mary received the message for the parish at the Thursday evening prayer group.

Mary has made two recent changes in her life: deciding to live alone (Jesus, she felt wanted to work some things out with her alone), and taking up the position of co-ordinator in a new parish project. This is the pre-school; seventy children attend. Mary spoke at the end of each Mass one Sunday in August, 1992, explaining the project and encouraging the parishioners to support the initiative. Now in full operation, the pre-school uses the program, <u>Catechesis of the Good Shepherd</u>. Without having heard of this program, Sister Lucy, entering the quiet room the program names 'the atrium', was stopped in her steps by the atmosphere of recollection and contemplative quiet. The program that Mary and her staff have chosen focuses on developing the relationship that exists between every small child and God. As a result, some children as young as two are leading their parents back to God.

At the Friday evening young adult prayer group, Mary frequently receives a message for the group, from our Lady or our Lord. At first, she ran away! But then she readied herself with pencil and paper to receive whatever they might say. Nothing happened. So she stopped waiting. Then on a Thursday when she was without anything to write, she was given a message during the rosary. When the group finished praying the rosary, Father Jack asked her what the message was. Startled that he knew, Mary immediately forgot what it was! Gradually she grows in quiet confidence.

Annie's life has changed completely. Before the dramatic intervention of Jesus and Mary in her life, Annie was outgoing and generous, but obstinate. Her marriage in 1984 to a Turkish Moslem student was opposed by all who knew her. But Annie idealistically went ahead with it. It was to end in separation after much grief. The annulment for which Annie asked was granted by the Church in February, 1991. Meanwhile our Lord asked her to share in some of the pains of His passion, and in the sorrow of His Mother's heart. As with some of the nine, she was often under attack by Satan who tried to terrify her away from this way of life. Standing by her always was Eric Fitch. They planned to marry if the annulment was granted; but shortly before the date they had fixed, Annie made a retreat and generously but mistakenly thought that giving all to her Lord meant giving up marriage and becoming a religious sister. When she telephoned to us to announce her decision to enter a convent, Eric was beside her, saying that he was ready for whatever God asked. Later, Annie came to see Christian marriage as God's plan for her, her calling. She and Eric were married in February, 1992.

At the Southern California Charismatic Conference in Anaheim in 1991, Annie met Father Robert De Grandis, who has a world-wide healing ministry. Annie and Eric now work with him, especially in praying for healing, travelling widely in the United States and abroad.

Extracts from Teachings given by Our Lady to Annie

Treat (all people) with love, kindness, tenderness and respect. Listen with the loving ears and merciful heart of my beloved Jesus. Be compassionate. Be humble. Gently, ever so gently and tenderly guide them back to the loving and merciful heart of my beloved Jesus. Do not teach with arrogance - but through your humble and loving words and actions. With love, - with <u>true</u> love - <u>all</u> of my little ones can be brought back. ... Pray before you speak - ask the Holy Spirit to fill you and speak His words of wisdom through you. (November 7, 1989)

My dear precious child, I am so glad, so happy, so joy-filled that you wished to come to me and to my Jesus for the strength, knowledge, courage, patience, humility and obedience that you are seeking. My child, the seeds of all these virtues lie within your soul - they simply need to grow. In order for them to grow you must pray - pray constantly. (September 7, 1989)

As you open your heart to Jesus more and more, you shall be filled with His peace and His love. You will have the happiness you have been searching for ... For when He is the center of your life, <u>all</u> shall be given to you. ... Live in the truth - live in the truth of my Jesus! Live in His love! ... His love is boundless, infinite, given to you freely without condition. (September 6 1989)

Extracts from Teachings given by Jesus to Annie

Be at peace; know of your nothingness before me; know of your insignificance. Yes, your soul is in an hour of darkness, but it will return to the light, the Light of my love. Despite the darkness, my little one, shine on! Shine brightly in the knowledge of my truth. Be assured of my love for you. (April 1, 1990)

(After Holy Communion) Do you feel the effusion of grace and love that I am pouring out into you? We are becoming fused together, one in body, mind, heart and soul! As we become one, receive also in fullness, my sufferings, my pains! Accept them, embrace them with total and complete love. (August 8, 1990)

Stefanie has reflected on the phenomena, at Scottsdale and other places, of Divine intervention in these days. She writes:

"With all the supernatural things happening - inner locutions, apparitions, healings - some people are offended and afraid. There are some extreme cases of malice, but mostly there are people who struggle with a purer heart and earnest desire to believe. A friend of mine is one of these - overloaded with stories of rosaries turning gold, spinning suns, apparitions, and inner locutions. Here is a person just coming back and trying to strengthen their conviction by discovering more and more how the call to conversion specifically applies to them, and confronted over and over with phenomena to which they cannot relate."

Stefanie questioned (as have the others in the group of nine, and surely all other visionaries in history), "Why Jesus, did you allow us to tell anyone what was happening to us?" "It came to me," Stefanie says, "that the only way we would accept the gift of silence is by experiencing first hand the difficulties a lack of silence causes for those around us. So far those around us who have been affected by this situation are primarily those called to be an integral part of our Lady's plan. For this reason they must learn what in them - fear, pride, envy, other things - causes them to have such a difficulty, because they will surely be exposed, often first hand, to the many gifts God wishes to bestow through our blessed Mother. Jesus asks for discipline. To discipline our speech is difficult, partly due to pride, and also largely because of the desire to share with a 'tangible' person the joy that fills one's heart and soul upon the receipt of such gifts." It is the speaking with another tangible person about the gifts which grounds them as it were, in reality, Stefanie reflects, more so than speaking to Jesus about them.

This is a predicament, and Stefanie longs for us to understand it: "It is not easy," she says, "to accept such gifts. One
must abandon many facets of personal control to rely totally
on Jesus who is leading us into a realm of prayer we do not
understand and never dreamed of experiencing. Trust in our
Lord is so severely tested. People experiencing these gifts
need to learn to clamp those lips together. I am seeing more
and more that we must only speak when spoken to with
regard to any supernatural phenomena, and even then we
must be modest in what we say. People often ask before they
are ready to accept that such graces are true, and unfortu-
nately we don't find out until later that they had trials because
of what they heard in response to their question. This is pride
on the part of the person asking and carelessness on the part
of the person answering. That is why our Lady said that we
should answer only the questions posed to us, saying no more
and no less than is required to answer the question." Stefanie's
reflections have brought her to the classical teaching of the
saints regarding extraordinary gifts: "I am seeing more and
more", she writes "that if we receive particular gifts, we
should thank Jesus, put them out of our minds until He calls
us to use them, and mentally and emotionally move on to the
other tasks that fill our day."

In early 1992, Sister Lucy left a message on **Susan**'s
telephone answering machine to say that she would be at the
morning eight o'clock Mass at Saint Maria Goretti church.
Susan had already left for that Mass; our Lady had told her to

be there! A bad headache that day did not deter her from following through whatever our Lady wished. Recently Susan had undergone ear surgery to relieve pressure in her ear, an operation that very few surgeons will perform. Then, in 1992, she went to Europe on pilgrimage to Lourdes and to other shrines. The days of exposure to fumes and to cigarette smoke caused a complete loss of hearing in one ear. Specialists said the condition was irreversible; but Susan says some hearing is beginning to return.

A great joy to Susan has been her small dog Joshua who alerts her to callers, as she is unable to hear the door bell. Since Joshua has sometimes to be left alone, Susan acquired a companion for him - a minute bundle of white fur she has named 'Charity'. Charity makes up in character what she lacks in size.

Perhaps it is partly her deafness that leads Susan to say that she cannot emphasize enough the importance of <u>listening</u> - of listening to hear our Lord speak in the depth of our hearts - not necessarily audibly. Mary Cook is of the same opinion - that we should clear our minds and allow Him to speak in whatever way. Mary says that we all have that gift of hearing Jesus, but that it is easily lost. Susan observes that we can reject a message that we hear, saying 'no'; but that if we do not listen, we cannot be obedient. If we ask a question of the Lord, she says, we should listen for a reply. It will come, and it will come again and again from all sides. <u>Listen with your heart; see and hear with your heart</u>. "If, for example," Susan says, "Our Lady says 'I love you', pray for the enlightenment of the Holy Spirit to come and enlighten this message, so simple yet so profound." "How important the Holy Spirit is," she adds, "in our walk, our journey towards heaven."

Our Lord has shown Susan how much honor we should give to our Lady. She says He has shown her so much about His Mother, that she cannot put into words the honor that is due to Mary. She, says Susan, is the one who has led her, and Susan is grateful.

Susan was blessed in her gift of listening, as other people have been, on one occasion by hearing the singing of a choir of angels. At Mass, during the singing of the Our Father, she heard the angelic music with her deaf ear.

Susan has had, as have all the nine, the promise of seeing our Lady; but in 1987 she was asked if she would make the sacrifice of not seeing her. This is a temporary sacrifice. In her opinion, those who love our Lord and go through trials without ever seeing anything are the real saints. She says she does not have visions or apparitions, though she can feel the presence of our Lady, or for example, of an angel. But as a child she saw Jesus coming on a cloud, arms outstretched. She believes that we can see our Lord and our Lady with our interior sight, that we can feel Jesus within ourselves.

Frequently groups ask Susan to speak to them. She goes if she is well enough. Our Lord has told her: "You will lead many people to me" (not to herself, she emphasizes). She shares what our Lord has given her, if she is asked. Her talks are, she says, simple. "Everything is so simple with the Lord, no worry, anxiety or fear. Our Lord says simplicity is the opposite of complexity." "What is complexity?" she asks. "Greed, selfishness - all the things that block us from our Lord, block us from being simple. Then our emotions, our sufferings lead us away." "What" she asks "are the virtues of our Lord? To love, to have mercy and compassion, to be joyful, humble. This is the gospel message He wants us to live: our Lord wants to be compassionate, merciful to others through us. Satan wants to inflict pain on others through us."

During the last two years, Sister Lucy has had the pleasure of meeting the parents of some of the nine: Annie's father and mother Dick and Judy Ross; Gianna's parents Jack and Tecla Talone; Susan's mother Dawn; and in the summer of 1992, Terry, mother of Wendy and Steve Nelson. Each modestly, but in complete faith, acknowledges the Lord's choice of their children.

Gianna's mother recounts incidents in which Gianna's life was threatened from before birth onwards, as though the destruction of the child was important to Satan. Gianna was as a child, as now, vivacious, joyful, gifted. When she was five her astonished parents found her putting on an accomplished ventriloquist act with a Beatle doll! They bought her her own doll, Alfie (whom she still has), and the small Gianna turned professional. A leading Hollywood agency signed her on after her success at a dance academy in ballet, tap-dancing, and singing. Normally the lower age limit of their signings was eighteen. Gianna was ten, but child stars were needed to dance with famous names whom Gianna does not wish us to mention. So many requests were made that the Talone family moved to Beverley Hills.

Television series, commercials, fashion modelling, for all these Gianna was in demand. She and Claudia, her older sister were nine and eleven year old escorts receiving guests at the Convention Ball when President Reagan was Governor of California. But not all was glamour in Beverley Hills. The local Bishop gave Gianna and Claudia free schooling in the Catholic school, while her mother re-paid him by teaching there. But the family were regarded as 'poor' by other pupils and staff. There were discrimination and ridicule. Gianna did not tell her mother because she was afraid of losing her friends. Gianna's mother says that her daughter would not go against people because she wanted to keep them as friends - a character trait which Gianna acknowledges. One day at school, when she was thirteen years old, Gianna was witness to a fight between two boys one of whom was pushed over the stair rail. Gianna leaped across the stairwell to save him. She was given a citation by the Governor of California for saving a life.

It was Gianna herself who began to realize that her life at that time was not what she wanted. At her request the family moved back to Arizona. Success followed her there as she became Miss Arizona Teenager and runner up for Miss National Teenager. She was a straight A student and winner of a scholarship to the University of California at Los Angeles being one of only ten students accepted for Drama. But within a short time she knew this was not her future. She changed her major to chemistry but put her theatrical skills to work for handicapped children. She read to the blind and put on shows for retarded children, taking Alfie along to entertain and teach them. The University took note, and Gianna, President of her class, was awarded a trophy as "Congeniality Student of the Year" and a bronze plaque for "Outstanding Achievement in Community Service". This is an award not given every year, only when merited. Gianna received it for an outreach program that she designed and which is still in use.

The Lord was tugging at her heart and now began putting obstacles in her path so as to divert her to His chosen ways. In her application for Medical School she scored eleven marks out of twelve (eight being the average, and nine considered good), but she was unsuccessful at every interview. Had she gone on to that training, her life would not have taken its present course.

Today, without a job, her marriage ended, derided by some who watched her on television, Gianna knows the worth of popularity and 'success'. She is currently working on a project called "Mission of Mercy", a mobile clinic for the poor and homeless, especially the elderly. Sixteen physicians and nurses are ready to staff it, and Gianna is raising money in a quiet way for the equipment. On going to register the name "Mission of Mercy", she found it was already taken. But the lady whose organization was using the name died, and so it was released to Gianna's project. Other organizations are interested, and if Mission of Mercy is a success, a national network will be formed.

Another project is a lay community for which our Lord asked. Gianna fought against the idea but capitulated in February, 1992, during a visit to Rome. The community would consist of single men and women, married couples, and possibly, eventually, religious. Just now fifteen adults are making an initial discernment. Already associates have asked to be affiliated from as far as New York and Virginia.

Father Jack Spaulding says that usually our Lady is sent by Jesus to the places in which she appears; but in Scottsdale, in his opinion, she comes because her Son Jesus is there. Mary never leads us to herself, but only to Jesus. This is one of the authentic signs of her presence. At Saint Maria Goretti parish, Mary is not the center. The life of the parish centers on the Mass, and Jesus adored in the Eucharist and radiates from this source.

If Jesus has in this unprecedented way come to an American parish, can we fail to listen to what He has come to say? We may be people who are "not into apparitions". But we are "into" the message of Scripture, the good news of Jesus whose first preached words were

THE TIME IS FULFILLED
THE REIGN OF GOD HAS DRAWN NEAR
BE CONVERTED AND BELIEVE THE
GOOD NEWS. (Mark 1:15)

Be converted, repent, as some translations say, just literally means "turn round" - turn to face God. And what shall we see when we are face to face with the Living God? Divine Mercy and Love. This is the good news. It is because of this good news that the Mother of God says she has come to Scottsdale, to America, as our Lady of Joy and of Mercy. "God is love" (1 John 4:8), and "His mercy is above all His works" (Psalm 145:9).

- III -
Prophetic Messages Through Stefanie: The Call to Conversion

Between mid-May and late October, 1989, Stefanie Staab received ten messages from Jesus. He did not appear to her. He dictated these messages to her quite clearly, verbally and interiorly, and told her to write them down. In mid-March, 1992, on Jesus's explicit instructions, Stefanie gave a copy of the messages to Father Robert Faricy. And about a week after that, Jesus gave her an eleventh message.

Stefanie's messages began to come to her in late August, 1988. One Sunday after Mass, on her way to go home, she felt that she just could not go home. She remained sitting in her car, and began to listen to jazz music on the car tape player. She knew then that she had to get a notebook. She bought a notebook and went home, thinking that she would write about conversions.

When she began to write, nothing came. Then she felt a strong presence, energy like electricity. And words began to come in a great rush of dictation, like a rollercoaster. Frightened, she went to Father Jack Spaulding, telling him that a voice had said these things to her and she had written them down.

Since then Stefanie has received many messages. Some are personal, for her only, some are for other persons. Usually the Lord or our Lady dictates them when Stefanie prays alone before the blessed Sacrament. Whenever the message begins, "Children of the world" or "My dear children", she knows that the message is for all and for some kind of publication.

This chapter gives, with little comment, the eleven messages, each one a strong prophetic call to conversion. Certainly the messages do not reflect Stefanie's personality. Joyful, happy, upbeat, and gentle, Stefanie seems an unlikely person to receive such messages. A reluctant prophet, she simply wrote what the Lord told her to write and then passed the words on to the man that the Lord indicated to her.

These prophecies stand in the tradition of the Old and New Testaments. They do not mean to frighten us but to call us to repentance, to urge us to turn from sin and to turn to the Lord. Spoken first to Stefanie, but to each of us, for us, their tone and form encourage us to read them slowly and to take them seriously.

On May 18, 1989, Jesus instructed Stefanie to write these words to us from Him: "Children of the world, heed my call. The time of my coming is sooner than you desire to believe. It is I, Jesus Christ, who am the Emissary of Mercy to the world, but you do not heed my call. My dear ones, read the Scriptures and open your hearts! I am making use of this servant to call you to repentance. Remember that the Baptizer came before me into the world to challenge my people. I now send to you those whom my Mother has selected to challenge you. You say to yourselves, 'They are religious fanatics; they are crazy; they are being led by deceptions of the evil one.' I tell you, look at their lives, the lives of those called to spread the words of my new gospel. They are not perfect; they are sinful, but they are abandoning all else to be at my service and, at my request, at the service of my dear Mother.

"The time has come for the prophecies to begin to be fulfilled. Listen to the children for they desire your salvation. Do not be envious or judgmental. Realize that all are called to be as children. Soon you shall be called to answer for the arrogance of this world - the arrogance that defies my Father, misuses His gifts, and abuses His creations. Listen to my words; listen to my words."

The second message, dated November 3, 1989, in some way balances the first. This message speaks more about love and about salvation, and talks about the salvation of those who do not know Jesus.

"I, the Lord, your God, care about your every emotion, your every desire. None who turn to me shall hunger for love or guidance. My Father, loving me, wishes glory for me and so He assigns souls to me. They are my sheep. Such is my love for my virgin Mother that I assign souls to be her children, her servants. Woe to those who say they are mine but criticize my Mother!

"You think my cross was made of wood! My cross is of sorrow, sorrow for your sins, sorrow for your rejection, sorrow for the hurt you cause to yourselves and to my other sheep.

"Are you so naive and so full of your own ego to think there is only one way to holiness? I, the Lord your God, tell you there is not. Why did I come to save Israel? I came because they loved not my Father. For those who love my Father but know not of me there is salvation. Who am I even, the Son of Man, to bar one from Paradise for not knowing me? If not even the Son of Man does so, how do you believe that you may do so? 'Woe,' I say to the accuser of Jews. They are my Father's chosen. I am the Light because I am one with the Father; those who love and obey the Father are mine as they are His. We are One.

"My dear Christian lambs, do not fool yourselves with arrogance. I say, 'Let all come to Heaven who honor my Father,' just as my Father says, 'Let all come to Heaven who honor my Son.'"

The third message, given June 3, 1989, from Jesus for us through Stefanie calls us to repentance and speaks about abortion. "My children of the Americas and of the world, listen to me, your Lord, as I call you to repentance. My dear, dear children, it is with great sorrow that I make this plea. You are so far from me. You must recognize your sins before you will open your hearts and your wills to repentance and conversion.

"Abortion. I wish to speak of abortion. How dare you take into your own hands the decision of life! This is my Father's right alone. You, in your arrogance, have decided on the timing of so many of my Father's gifts to you. How dare you tell the Creator when and how to create! Not only have you become arrogant in your dealings with one another but also in your dealings with God, our Almighty Father! Listen as I tell you, you who sit debating the merits of physical life; debate the merits of spiritual life, the life of the soul, not the body. It is by your sins that these souls are denied the right to sanctification through human life. By my Father's mercy they are taken to my Mother's side and to her feet so that they may receive the love that you, in your selfishness, deny them.

"Do you think that a body without normal physical functions ceases to be a vessel of the Holy Spirit, the conveyor of a soul through life? You are wrong, it does not. The body is a gift from God to grant mobility to the soul. If God creates a soul for the purpose of praising Him interiorly in a way that does not require physical or mental aptitude, who is man to decide 'No' about life for this child?

"This is the sin that my sacred Heart demands repentance for and that my Mother's most immaculate Heart grieves over. Turn to me and away from this wickedness, and I shall give you strength to be able to love your children as God the Father loves you, without condition, without qualifying. Hear my call, oh children of the New Covenant."

Three days later, the Lord asked Stefanie to write these words that call us to turn to Jesus and the Father and that speak of Jesus' Mother. It is clear that the Lord speaks to all - to all Christians and also to non-Christians.

"Children of the world, hear my call. There are so many areas of your lives in which you have lulled yourselves into complacency by false hopes and expectations. This is why you are so captivated by sin, sinful ways, sinful thinking.

"I tell you the answer is prayer. So many of you pray hoping that God the Father will come from without to answer you. Look within. Within you is your soul, and it is your souls with whom God, my Father, communicates. Your souls are so weak from neglect. You do not exercise them as you exercise your bodies, and which is most transient? Do you consider this thought?

"I long so for my children to return to me and my Father. Return to us now before it is too late for you to do so. Do you think my Mother has been permitted to appear and make her presence known in so many places for no significant reason? She is a symbol, the new Eve, and she shall reign as queen above men and Earth. Follow her. If you are Protestant, follow her example of purity and chastity. She shall lead you home simply by example. For those whom I have called to know her well, keep her company. My Mother loves all of you, from any race, any religion, any background. Do you want to know how to turn from sin and repent? Follow my Mother, I tell you. She will lead you to me by our divine union which shall never be broken. Amen, my children, amen; exercise your souls allowing my Mother's love for you to be your guide and support."

The next day, June 7, Jesus spoke to Stefanie, speaks to us now through her, about divorce. "My children of the world, are you so surprised that I bring my words to you in this way? I shall work in many ways to call my children home to me and into my Father's hands. Tonight I will speak on divorce. So many of you suffer this pain, this awful pain. There are two reasons.

"Often, because of the condition of your souls, you do not wait for me to lead you and so you are unhappily matched. This is when sadness overcomes me because my children ignore my goodness by not seeking my counsel. Another reason is the lack of maturity and commitment and love. Do you know why I unite a man and a woman? I unite them to become one, forever. Forever they are souls in union with one another and God. So much praise can come to my Father through this holy union, the sacred journey of two sacred parts. And yet, you contaminate this beauty with greed, avarice, and lust. You greed over one another's time, affection, and bodies. I tell you, love one another to the deepest parts of your hearts and souls. In those depths you shall find God the Father.

"Marriage is the beginning of physical life. It is the vehicle through which God the Father unites His people and creates His children. God gives to you this call and yet you are selfish with its fruits. You do not want babies; you do not want unconditional love; you do not want intimacy of the soul. You do not want these fruits because you are afraid and therefore unwilling to give — selfish, prideful, shallow. Why can you not accept my Father's beautiful gifts? Has evil got you so fooled by worldly issues? Lay bare your souls, and marriages shall become sacred to me, to my Father, and to you."

Less than a week later, on June 12, Jesus spoke again about divorce. "My dear children, again I beckon to you, 'Hear my call!' So absorbed by worldly desires are you that you forsake those things of God which are inconvenient to you. This why you have allowed divorce and abortion to run rampant. Divorce is the sin I wish to address today also. You who are married must bond together your gifts. How shall this be done when you do not know me? I am the source. My dear ones, do you pray to know what gifts you have to offer your husband or your wife? No, you pray that he or she shall offer more to you. Give up your selfish ways. There is no room for them in such a union of God. What I ask is that you pray for enlightenment each day to show you what you may give your husband or your wife. The attitude of selfishness between husband and wife has opened the door for so many other sins. The sins of sexuality come from this attitude and from them the sin of abortion and on it goes, the sin becoming more and more complete in this selfishness.

"When I say bare your souls to one another I mean bare them in offering, not in request for healing. The way is unconditional love and trust in God. My Father has a plan for each soul. Forsake not my Father's work which must occur through you. My dear one, examine your consciences and then approach one another in love, unselfish love."

One week later, Jesus speaks through Stefanie particularly to people who are well off and who have some power in the world. "My dearest children of the world, hear my call. Harken unto me. You who are mighty counsel the poor. You counsel them through many media. You counsel them through your appearance; you counsel through your attitude; and most of all you counsel them by your example of materialism. I tell you the day shall soon come when you shall lose these possessions; and the poor shall counsel you, but not with appearance, attitude, or advertising. With love they shall counsel you and have pity on you.

" Yes, I say 'pity' because how pitiful you mighty ones of the world shall be. You may receive mercy only if you will accept it. Can you accept mercy? Learn, I implore you. If you do not learn to accept my mercy, you shall be doomed. Your only remaining vehicle to carry you to Heaven is the loving arms of my mercy. Those who are proud, haughty, and overly independent of their brothers and sisters shall receive no mercy. Is this because I wish not to give mercy?

"No, I tell you it is you who wish not to receive mercy at the hands of your brothers and sisters. My children may ask why does the Lord come to you over and over with the same message, the one that began with my gospels? I tell you it is my mercy, that rare gem that shall bring you salvation. It is a rare gem I place in your path; do not, I warn you, step over it. I love you, even the most haughty and arrogant of you. Know that I, the Lord and your true God, love you so very much. Humble yourselves before me and my holy ones around you, and you shall receive the gem of my mercy. Hear my call my dear ones, my scattered ones, and answer me! Amen."

The next week, Stefanie received a message in which the Lord begs us to turn to him humbly. "Children of the world, hear my call! It is the Lord, God, Jesus Christ, who comes to you in all humility to beg for your love, for your response to my sacrifice of love for you. Humility. Humility is what is lacking in your society today. I came into your world at a time when humility was lost to my Father's chosen people. Now it is lost to mine. Oh my dear ones, my sheep, follow me on the way toward humility and sacrifice. You shall open your hearts and souls in this way. Tell me, 'Lord, I am tired of arrogance, selfishness, greed, and pride. I desire Your ways, oh Lord!' Tell me this, my dear ones, and I shall make it possible for you. I do not ask you to convert your hearts and change your lives and then come to me. On the contrary, I say to you, 'Come to me as you are. If you are divorced, come to me; if you have rejected the children sent by my Father, come to me; if lust plagues your mind and your heart, come to me!' I am the source of the cleansing waters, the purifying blood that begot your salvation. I am the source of light for dark souls. I tell you of your sins not that you might hang your heads in shame never to approach my purity. No, my children, my sheep, I call you to me so that your shamefully lowered heads may be raised to me, and so that my light may shine upon you, through your face and permeate your heart and soul. Know your sinfulness, yes; but also and most importantly, know me. For I am your hope.

"Peace to you, my children who have heard my call and turned your faces to me. I shall come for you on the judgment day. Amen."

Stefanie received another message about two weeks later, July 9, 1989. Giving more a teaching than a prophecy, Jesus talks about Mary and Joseph and who they are for us. "So many know not of the purity of my Mother's virginity. Even my apostles knew not this rare and true gem, a one of a kind gem, created as the only gem of its kind in the universe. Why, you ask was this not contained in my gospels? You are beginning to understand. My visit to Earth was not the end of my work; it was not the whole of my mission. It was simply the beginning. My Mother is united with me in that we are Co-redeemers, partners if you will, in one mission. Why did God choose a Mother and Son? Because the purity of the relationship in human terms causes it to be beyond the suspicion Satan chooses to create. If we had been husband and wife, God's purity, His chastity in us, would have been suspect. Why do you think speculation was cast by the evil one on my pure and holy relationship with Mary Magdalene - the beauty of the repentant sinner before her God, basking in His love and forgiveness: Satan wishes to desecrate this vision of hope. Also suspect is the relationship between my beloved step-father Joseph and my dear Mother, the holy one. How dare the relationship conceived wholly by God, the Almighty Father, be questioned thusly. They became the holy ones, not I; I am God, God made flesh, with the perfection of His divinity pulsing through my veins. I pay homage with love and respect to these two dear humans who magnified and glorified my eternal Father. I solemnly tell you, my dear one, and I wish the world to know, that I, the King of Kings, the second Person of the Blessed Trinity, accept those who honor and venerate Joseph and Mary, the Pure Lily of God and her earthly protector, a truly just man.

"The world must know the glory of God present in these two holy beings and must imitate their virtues: holiness, obedience, chastity, love — the love of Heaven in its purity. The time has come, for the Son has glorified the Father; and now with the Father He shall glorify the holy ones, and they are Joseph, the saint of men, and Mary, the purity and rectification of all women. All those who follow these ones in the path to holiness follow me toward my eternal Father, becoming once again His, in spirit, mind, body, and soul."

July 22, 1989, the Lord said, says to us now through Stefanie, "My dear followers, heed not the way of the world. Heed only my divine call. I call you to grace, to hope, charity, faith, love, joy, wisdom, compassion, courage, and all the virtues of the Holy Spirit of my Father. I, your Lord, love you and invite you to return to me, my ways, my peace, and my purpose. Give glory to my Father, honor to my Mother, and Heaven shall be yours. Heed my call; it is the call of my love and my mercy. Bless you who have responded. Go out to those who have not; you have my blessings."

The Lord dictated two more prophetic messages to Stefanie. When he told her to give all these messages to Father Faricy, Stefanie searched the house for them but could not find them all. Two of these messages are still missing. Then, in mid-March, 1992, Jesus told Stefanie not to worry and not to look any more. He gave her the following message to substitute for the ones she lost.

"My dear children of the world, hear my call. I call you to life through death. I call you to love through suffering. I call you to joy through self-denial. Follow me and I shall bring to you eternal bliss. This is my call. This is my offering. This is my glorious work for my Father, with whom I am one. I tell you now to follow my Mother for she leads all to me. She is love, comfort, compassion, personified in one who is human. Doubt not her purpose. Doubt not her plan. Doubt not her love.

"All who come to me shall know the joy of heaven. All who come to me in the loving arms of my Mother shall know also the bliss on earth of motherly consolation and tender prompting to the glory of God. Amen I say to you, my children of the world. Alleluia. Amen. Be it done according to my Father's will."

- IV -
Prophetic Messages Through Gianna: The Mercy of God

Gianna Talone, small, attractive, intelligent, vivacious, with a doctorate in pharmacology, until recently head of pharmacology at Saint Joseph's Hospital in Phoenix, took a leave of absence from her work to spend several weeks in the summer of 1992, from mid July to late August, in the cloistered Carmelite Monastery of the Sacred Heart, Hudson, Wisconsin, near Saint Paul, Minnesota. There, she lived the same life as the contemplative sisters, praying, working, and participating in all aspects of community life.

In many ways this was a difficult time for Gianna, a time for growing in humility and self-knowledge. Her prayer was dark and dry. Near the end of her stay, the convent dog bit her face, and she required medical treatment, including some plastic surgery.

Our Lady, as always, appeared to her and spoke to her every evening. Gianna told the Mother Superior and the Prioress, both, about the apparitions; but the other sisters did not know.

And Jesus spoke to her often, giving her each day one "lesson" for eventual publication. These lessons continued to come after Gianna returned to Scottsdale in time for the

Thursday, August 27, prayer meeting at Saint Maria Goretti parish. Partly because of the publication of two books on the Scottsdale events in the spring of 1992, one by Rene Laurentin and one by us,[1] along with local television coverage and a televised interview with Gianna the same spring, the apparitions at Scottsdale became much better known. Even larger crowds now attend the Thursday evening prayer and Mass. Saint Joseph's Hospital in Phoenix terminated Gianna's position there just before she left the monastery.

The Riehle Foundation of Milford, Ohio, publishes the lessons that Jesus gives to Gianna, each one a few pages, in several volumes.[2] At the time of writing this book, the sixth and probably final [according to Gianna] volume has not yet appeared.

Here are three of the lessons, from the sixth set of lessons that Gianna has received from Jesus, a set not yet all received and not yet published in September, 1992. Gianna has given us permission to include them in this chapter.

We want to point out that Jesus dictates these lessons to Gianna not just for her, but for publication - that is, for all of us and, in particular, for each one of us.

---

1   *Our Lord and Our Lady in Scottsdale*, Rene Laurentin (Faith Publishing Company, Milford, Ohio, 1992) and *Our Lady Comes to Scottsdale: Is It Authentic?*, Robert Faricy, S.J., Lucy Rooney, S.N.D.de N. (The Riehle Foundation, Milford, Ohio, 1991)

2   *I Am Your Jesus of Mercy* Volumes I to V (The Riehle Foundation, Milford, Ohio, 1989 to 1992)

St. Maria Garetti Church

The Blessed Sacrament Chapel at St. Maria Garetti is called "The Tabernacle" where the adoring Angels hold candles and surround the Crucifix which cradles the Hosts.

Outside view of the Blessed Sacrament Chapel.

The Crucifix above the alter in St. Maria Garette Church.

Satue of Our Lord in Church – sculptor Carlos Ayla.

Statue of Our Lady in St. Maria Goretti Church — Sculptor Carlos Ayla

Fr. Jack Spaulding. Pastor of St. Maria Goretti and Spiritual Guide.

Gianna during an apparition.

Sr. Lucy Rooney, S.N.D. de N.; Alfie and Gianna.

Stefanie and Gianna.

Susan.

Wendy and Mary

Steve with his wife Susan.

Fr. Bob Faricy, S.J.; Erick Fitch; Annie; Fr. Bob De Grandis, S.S.J.

Our Lady appears to Annie during her marriage to Eric Fitch.

The happy couple, Annie and Eric, married Feb. 17, 1992.

Annie with her parents, Dick and Judy Ross.

Lesson 35, received July 21, 1992

My dear little one, do ordinary things with extraordinary love. Have fidelity in the little things you do. Be at peace, and believe with all your heart my love for you and that I am by your side.

Everything you do, do it as if it were for me. Be proficient yet gentle. Touch everything with an <u>extraordinary</u> love. This is how in your ordinariness you become extraordinary. You must believe in me and trust so fervently in me to be able to see me in everything and everyone. If you see me in everything and everyone, you will be loving, gentle, and kind, if you love me ... Take the time to do all your chores and recreation with extraordinary love ... Take the loving "touch of love" to all your works and be a follower of <u>extraordinary love</u>.

The people of your world are hastily working, and take care only of the things they perceive as meaningful. But all is meaningful if I have created all. Do not select only that which you have desired to love.

Take time and love the small works you do. You will find much joy and peace when you devote extraordinary love in the ordinary tasks, the small jobs done on a daily basis. If you can take care of the small items, then you will be able to love and tend to the bigger projects <u>with</u> the <u>same</u> love. This extraordinary love will become your way, and you will live in union with me.

The way you treat one another no matter what position or title in life you hold: you will be of the same love if you start to love all, the weak and the strong, with a gentle, extraordinary care. I love you all and only desire your love to live in union with the holy Trinity. My words are for you because my love is for you. I am because of you. Because of you my Father sent me. He loves you. I am for you.

Lesson 45, received August 1, 1992:

My dear one, do not be caught up in yourself, because it will only hinder your growth. There is a difference between loving yourself and being self centered. You need to empty yourself continually, abandoning yourself to the will of God.

Do not chase after the things of this world; chase only heavenly desires, for everything will perish that is of the world. The more you strip yourself of your own will, the more you can sincerely give more of yourself to one another. Let go of those things you hold bound. Let yourself be free, and you will be free of heart. Then all your oppressions will vanish, your fear will disappear, and you will experience the joy of purity and intimacy.

Do not worry what people say about you. Remember, I can deliver you from any circumstance that would harm you. There is no need to worry what someone will say about you. Everyone must answer to me for their actions. Anyone who hurts you will only hurt themselves. Do not waste energy on those who harbor hatred and are your enemies because of envy and jealousy. If you exert your energy trying to gain the acceptance of your enemies by pleasing them, you will always lose. They will only sidetrack and use you for their gain. This is not an act of mercy for you.

Be giving to those open to receive. Be giving to those who cannot give, and be giving to those who are not willing to receive but have a clean heart. ...

So never be afraid of what others say to you. Simply keep your focus on me. Do not worry if you experience defeat; I will take care of you and deliver you to freedom. Trust in me. You wish to trust in yourself over trusting in me. Those who love the things of this world apart from me gain nothing and do not know anything of truth or wisdom.

I am with you in all your suffering. Persist and do not give up. Stand firm in your trust of me over the trust of yourself.

I want you to love yourself dearly. I want you to embrace yourself. There is no vision that is of so great importance that it would supersede the love I want you to have of yourself. In this way you love me. I want this for all my people. I do not desire you to be self centered, seeking and chasing the things of this world, but I do desire you to love yourself purely and keeping me in sight, surrendering and continually emptying yourself to follow the way of <u>love, truth, hope, and mercy</u>. Bless you, my dear people. Be at peace.

Lesson received March 3, 1992. (Jesus dictated this lesson to Gianna especially for this book, and indicated that it was to be the final lesson of the sixth and as yet unpublished set.)

My dear little one, it is time to write down my words about mercy. As I have said, mercy is the divine power of my love which flows out to those in need. In order to discuss mercy it is first necessary to speak of love, for you cannot be merciful unless you love.

I am love. You love because I first loved. I am love and he who abides in love abides in me and me in him. It is not that you have loved that my Father sent me as an offering for your sins, but it is because my Father loves you and is love. I am one with the Father. Because of Him therefore I am.

Nothing is sweeter than love because love proceeds from the Father and cannot rest but in Him. If you want to have mercy on someone, you need to love that person and be compassionate. If you want mercy in return, you need to allow yourself to be loved ... My love has no measure. My love feels no burden and values no labors. My love is free of all worldly affections.

You are weak in love and imperfect in virtue and are therefore in need of my comfort and strength. Because I am love and because my love is generous, I initiate and am the catalyzer for the great works you do. I am speaking to all my people as I am speaking to you. I excite in you the desire to seek that which is perfect. Love me more than yourself, and yourself only for me. Love all others in me who loves as the law of love commands.

Did I not say in Isaiah, "When you pass through the water, I will be with you; in the rivers you shall not drown. When you walk through fire, you shall not be burned; the flames shall not consume you"? ...

Love is gentleness, kindness, submissive thankfulness. Love keeps guard over all the senses. It is being chaste and sober and in union with fidelity. It is not intent upon vain things. Love is patient, courageous, prudent, long-suffering, and never seeking itself.

Remember, my dear one, that the Lord your God is God indeed, the faithful and loving God who keeps His merciful covenant down through the generations towards those who love Him. I am the Lord your God. Therefore you shall love me, your Lord, your God, with all your heart, all your soul, with all your mind, and with all your strength. And, my dear one, if I love my people so, you must have the same love for them.

How? If you love one another, I dwell in you and my love is brought to perfection in you. You say, "How can we love, if you don't dwell in us first?" I say you are because of me, and that you love because I first loved, because I am love.

However, in this journey of love you cannot think that you will never feel any trouble nor suffer any grief of heart or pain of the body. This is not the state of this present life but of the bliss of everlasting rest. Nor should you feel especially loved if you experience love. The progress and perfection in a true lover of virtue does not consist of feelings. The true virtue of love is offering your whole self to the will of God, not seeking consolation in things little or great, or of things of yourself. If you are overcome with suffering, do not think you ought not to suffer; but know that when the interior comfort is withdrawn that you walk in the true and right way of peace [no matter how dark] and can hope without doubt that you will see my face with great joy.

Let us talk about suffering and forgiveness, my little one, because in order to understand mercy you must understand suffering and be forgiving of others. When you suffer injustice or endure hardship in an awareness of my presence, this is my grace working in you. In suffering you submerge yourself into my abandonment, and salvation results through my mercy. Suffering is most painful, yet the ultimate proof of your faith in God.

Suffering which is interior is the most valuable suffering because it is the suffering man cannot see with his eyes, only with his heart. It is union with me when you see suffering with your heart, and it allows you to be merciful. It allows you to love through compassion. When you can unite with your brethren in harmony and compassion, you are uniting in love and mercy. You are in union with me.

As for forgiveness, I have told you to trust in me, your Lord God, and I will help you. I have said, "Do not judge and you will not be judged; pardon and you shall be pardoned." "Get rid of all bitterness, all passion and anger, harsh words, slander, and malice." Be kind, forgiving, and compassionate. Forgive as I have forgiven you, and you will receive my divine merciful love. Love and mercy cannot exist where there is division.

Forgive yourself so I can forgive you. Do not harbor negative condemnations against yourself. Love yourself; be merciful to your own self. Be compassionate. If you cannot forgive without expectations, you cannot have a pure heart. Mercy is related to forgiveness.

Now I need to continue on the subject of reconciliation, because in order for me to shed my mercy, you must reconcile. Use the sacrament of reconciliation. Sin will continuously stain the soul until you allow forgiveness from me <u>and</u> yourself. I cannot forgive you if you hold bound your sin by not forgiving yourself. The conflict and separation of inner being will exist until you allow my goodness to prevail. Reconciliation is needed to see me in your heart. A true confession will result from my Spirit's guidance and your sincerity, honesty, and humility. If you would humble yourself to accept the truth and allow me to unite my goodness to you, the joy would be overwhelming.

Now then child, let us speak on mercy. Mercy is love. Mercy is union with God. <u>Union with God is certainty of victory and eternal abundance of virtues, which lead to an</u>

eternal seat in the kingdom.

There are three ways to exercise mercy:
1. by deed,
2. by word,
3. by prayer.

Mercy is the unquestionable proof of love for me. I have said you cannot have mercy unless you love. Love never wrongs the neighbor, hence love is the fulfillment of the law [Romans, child]. Therefore, be merciful to your brother. Even if he has hurt you, have mercy on him.

What is justice? Is justice a standard set by man in retaliation for someone hurting someone else, or is justice that which is in the hands of my Father? The law of justice through man cannot take hold of you.

Know that everything that exists is enclosed in my mercy. My Father did not send me into the world to condemn it, but that you might be saved through me. Therefore, beloved, do not avenge yourselves. Leave that to God's wrath. If you sin, admit your guilt, ask for forgiveness, and return to me. Immerse yourselves in my mercy; I will redeem you.

Have mercy and compassion on your offenders. Pray for them and those of evil ways who tread with guilt. Pardon their sins, for the remnant of their inheritance is in my hands. Do not persist in anger or pass judgment. Have mercy.

If you are guilty, return to the Lord, and I will not turn away. Cleanse your hands; purify your hearts. Do not return evil with evil. Submit to me. Resist the evil one who tries to destroy love through your man-made law. It is your crimes that separate you from me.

You who say that you are merciful and loving then turn in judgment on someone and seal his fate, is that mercy? It is your sins that blind you and make you hide your face from me. Eventually all will pass from this world. At the moment of your last breath you will not have anything to defend you except my mercy. Mercy is love, and pure love gives the soul strength at the moment of dying. ... I will give you a new heart, replacing your cold one. Live under grace, not under the law.

You are weak in love and imperfect in virtue because you keep your distance from me. Then sin is committed; and you condemn others, leaving yourself with unclean lips living with others of unclean lips. Those who come to me and are merciful, I will look upon in their distress.

In conclusion, my little one, mercy is love. Those who love are merciful and are begotten of me. The greatest gift is love. I am love, and I am a gift to you from my Father. My Father loves you because He sent me to you.

Write now, child, I Corinthians 13: 1-8. "If I speak with human tongues, and angelic as well, but do not have love, I am a noisy gong, a clanging cymbal. If I have the gift of prophecy and, with full knowledge, comprehend all mysteries, if I have faith great enough to move mountains, but have not love, I am nothing. If I give everything I have to feed the poor and hand over my body to be burned, but have not love, I gain nothing.

"Love is patient; love is kind. Love is not jealous; it does not put on airs; it is not snobbish. Love is never rude; it is not self-seeking; it is not prone to anger; neither does it brood over injuries. Love does not rejoice in what is wrong but rejoices in the truth.

"There is no limit to love's forbearance, to its trust, its hope, its power to endure. Love <u>never</u> fails. Prophecies will cease, tongues will be silent, knowledge will pass away."

I will never pass away because I am love, and you will live in me always if you love, for <u>I am love and mercy.</u>

Gianna does not always attend the Friday night young adult prayer meeting. When she does, Jesus and Mary speak through her, as well as usually through at least one other person present.

When she is in Scottsdale, Gianna always goes to the Thursday night prayer meeting and Mass in the Saint Maria Goretti parish church. She has, up until recently, been the one to receive the message from our Lady. Annie Fitch, when present, for a long period of time also saw our Lady and heard the message. Mary Cook sees our Lady in an interior vision; she does not go into ecstasy as Gianna and Annie have always done during the apparitions, nor does she perceive our Lady in the same way as Gianna and Annie have. Mary Cook's experience of our Lady, however, seems to us just as authentic as that of Gianna and Annie. Normally Gianna writes the message; and the celebrant, usually Father Spaulding, reads it to the congregation that same evening at the conclusion of the rosary. When Gianna has gone outside Scottsdale and not come to the Thursday meetings, Annie Ross Fitch has written the message. When neither could be present, as happened for over two months in the summer of 1992 when Gianna was travelling and then in Wisconsin with the Carmelite sisters and after Annie had moved with her husband Eric to New Orleans, our Lady did not appear at the Thursday night meetings. Our Lady or Jesus spoke only during the homily through Father Jack Spaulding. Then the last Thursday in July and on the Thursdays after that, she has appeared to and given the message to Mary Cook, who has written it down to be read later before the Mass.

The messages given by our Lady on Thursday evenings, usually during the third joyful mystery of the rosary, before the celebration of the Mass, are brief, and they are for all of us.

The following are some of these messages, given recently by the Blessed Virgin Mary to Gianna for us:

Thursday, May 21, 1992

My dear little children, it brings me joy to see you praying. Pray! Pray! Pray! I take your prayers to Jesus who presents you to the Father. My dear ones, prayer is the powerful tool to prevent dissension and confusion from the evil one. My children, please unite. Do not look at the past, but unite now in the moment and going on from this point together. Do not try to control or be stubborn. These only bring self destruction, not spiritual freedom. I love you, little ones, and bless you in the name of my Son. Thank you for responding to my call.

Thursday, June 4, 1992

My dear children, Jesus loves you. He is my dear Son, my dear Jesus. In the midst of your world there are struggles and hardships, but all can be overcome because Jesus has overcome the world. ... All love is of Him, and all must be yielded to Him in love to live in union with Him in His peace. I bless you, my little ones, and I encourage you this night to give all of yourself to Jesus in commitment of love. There is nothing you risk when you give Him your total being as He has given to you. ... Thank you for your response. Peace can exist if you begin to live peacefully and unselfishly. Blessings in the name of Him who has sent me.

Thursday, June 11, 1992

My dear little children, peace to you and blessings in the name of my Son. My dear ones, I need to continue to invite you to daily prayer and to focus on my Son. Trust in Him, my little ones. All will be well, and you will live in His most sacred Heart if you love Him and allow H im to love you. Trust, my dear ones, and pray. Never cease praying. There is much destruction in the world, but Jesus is peace and love. ... I love you and bless you in the name of Jesus. Thank you for responding to my call.

The following Thursday, June 18, in the parish Church of Saint Joseph, Philadelphia, invited there to pray with a group from the parish, Gianna received this message from our Lady:

My dear little children, I am your Mother of Joy who comes in the blessing of my Son. My dear little ones, pray with all your heart. When you pray with your <u>heart</u>, do not merely recite your prayers. Sing love songs to my Son, who loves you. Love, my little ones; love, love, love one another. Unity and harmony are fruits of peace. I love you, and my Son's grace is upon you. Thank you for responding to my call. [Gianna, commenting on the apparition, said that our Lady, quite joyful, came with three baby angels, prayed together with Gianna and gave a special blessing to everyone there.]

At the conclusion of the Southern Californian Charismatic Conference at Anaheim, 1992, Father Rene Laurentin, one of the conference speakers, whose book on the Scottsdale events had just been published, persuaded Gianna who was at the conference to undergo various tests during one of our Lady's apparitions to her. Gianna reluctantly agreed. Tests were made at the University of California San Francisco Medical Center, in the presence of Father Laurentin and Father Bill Delaney, S.J. There were two doctors: Philip Loron who is French and German Doctor Yinsing. The latter is Chief of Staff of the Psychiatry Unit of the University of California at San Francisco.

Attached to various monitors and wearing a 'cap' of twenty electrodes on her head and eyes, Gianna waited, having no certainty that our Lady would appear. She began to pray and was told afterwards that her voice slowed down as she passed from an aware "beta" state to an "alpha" or passive state. Then her voice "disappeared", although she was obviously speaking with someone as the wave pattern returned to beta (in beta, but with an alpha carrier). The alpha state came again when our Lady left and Gianna knelt in recollection. During the eight minutes of the apparition, Gianna did not blink despite reflex tests and flashing of lights. Her eyes were open all the time. The ocular test is the most significant. The results showed nothing pathologically amiss; the tests indicated no epilepsy, hallucination, sleep disorder, hysteria or illusion.

Towards the end of her time of seclusion in the Carmelite monastery, Jesus indicated that He wanted Gianna back in Scottsdale in time to receive an important message on August 27. Word of this spread, and a larger than usual congregation assembled for the Thursday evening rosary and Mass. Our Lady appeared to Gianna during the rosary. This is the message our Lady gave to her for us:

Message from Our Lady to the World received by Gianna Talone, at Saint Maria Goretti Parish, Scottsdale, August 27, 1992

My dear children, I urge your close attention as my Son has allowed me to be here. Please, my little ones, put aside your falsehoods and fears. There is too much negativity acting as a catalyst to human destruction. I invite you instead to draw closer to one another in prayer. Renew prayer in your family and devotion to spending more time with Jesus. It is URGENT. There are great struggles about to unfold. Division in families is leading to divisions in the church. Reconciliation is URGENT. I have asked prayer, conversion, penance, and, initially, you took the steps to procure your relationship with God; but you are reverting to old ways. I have asked obedience to my Pope, but division is resulting. The need for prayer, reconciliation, harmony, love and conversion is <u>urgent NOW</u>! Renounce what is preventing you in your spiritual growth. Read the holy Scripture, and listen to the Holy Spirit speak the message of my Son.

Begin right now to solidify your relationship with God by loving yourselves and restoring your self-respect. Cease running from yourselves. You cannot love your countrymen if you do not love yourself. You are walking ways of power instead of love. The greatest sin is that which destroys love. This is URGENT. The effects of this wickedness are causing jealousy, hatred, killing and divisions. War, power struggles and economic warfare are surfacing from lack of love. My Son is tired, very tired. The faith of God is forgotten. The time is coming when every man and woman on this earth will know that God exists. All will have a glimpse of the state of their soul. Those seconds will seem an eternity. Your love of gold and silver is about to become glittering dust and be swept away.

Spiritual warfare exists in the heavens, and you must NOW live in the perfection of your faith. The wicked are convinced they are invisible, but they are not. Do not be afraid. To all his faithful ones God <u>promises</u> victory over the powers of evil and the world. Know my little ones, that only God can make you holy. You can receive God's seal on your soul only by abandoning your will to Him. God's love will shower you and replace everything, if you accept it. Bless you my little ones, and thank you for responding to my <u>urgent</u> call.

- V -
Annie and the Gifts of the Spirit

Annie Ross Fitch and her husband Eric Fitch moved from Scottsdale to New Orleans in the summer of 1992. Annie works full time in pastoral ministry, always with Eric, often with Father Robert De Grandis, praying with prayer groups, parish groups, Marian groups, and at religious conventions and conferences.

Although Annie attended the Friday night prayer group in the beginning, she stopped going long before she left Scottsdale. Instead she went to a small charismatic prayer group in Scottsdale's Ascension parish on Wednesday evenings. Going to the prayer group helped her to use the gifts of the Spirit, the charisms, that the Lord has given her, especially the gifts of word of knowledge, word of wisdom, discernment of spirits, and praying for all kinds of healing, physical and emotional and spiritual, and the gift of sometimes receiving personal messages from Jesus or Mary for the person with whom she is praying. In particular, Annie receives many words of knowledge when she prays with people. Very often, the person with whom she prays falls down, overcome by grace, and rests in the Spirit.

The 1991 annual Catholic charismatic convention over the Labor Day weekend in Anaheim, California, changed many things in Annie's life. She received the Baptism in the

Holy Spirit. The way she prays with people has changed radically. All shyness and timidity and lack of self confidence are gone since the convention, and she uses the gifts the Lord gives her without any inhibitions. Even at the convention, she was loath to raise her hands in prayer or to pray over people. The second day of the convention, Father Faricy asked her to go to the nursery room, where small children are taken care of while their parents attend the convention events, to pray over the children. She went, and she prayed over them extending her hands; it was a new and important experience for her, the first time that she had ever prayed over anyone out loud and spontaneously. Then she met Father De Grandis. He has since helped her.

At a convention workshop guided by Father Faricy, Sister Lucy Rooney, and Father De Grandis, while Gianna Talone was praying with people in the room, a new thing happened to Annie. Standing near the front of the room, she suddenly felt her hand shoot up in the air, as though in prayer over people, and a group of people in front of her suddenly fell down, all at once, overcome by the power of the Holy Spirit.

Since that Labor Day weekend in Anaheim, at the annual charismatic convention, the Word has taken on a new and great importance for her: not only God's word in the Bible, but also religious and spiritual books. She reads the Bible more, uses it more, and reads more in general, especially books of a spiritual and religious nature.

Annie no longer sees our Lady on a daily or a regular basis. She does see her often, in an interior way, in her soul, especially when she was in Scottsdale during the apparitions of our Lady on Thursday nights in Saint Maria Goretti church, but not the way that she did. She saw her in an exterior way, in an apparition, during her wedding Mass, celebrated by Father Robert De Grandis, at about 10:30 or 10:35, on February 17, 1992, at Our Lady of Perpetual Help church in Scottsdale, and then again on December 12, the feast of Our Lady of Guadalupe. Our Lord appeared to Annie three times in late November, 1991, once at the end of December, and once the Sunday after her wedding. Annie speaks daily, and often all day long with Jesus and Mary, and sometimes with Saint Teresa of Avila and Padre Pio.

Annie's health is good, but her hands and feet hurt all the time, especially on Friday, Saturday, and Sunday. She tries to act as normally as possible. Sometimes her hands ooze a watery oil. When that began while Annie and Eric were still in Scottsdale, she telephoned in panic to Father De Grandis in New Orleans and asked him what she should do. He told her to ask Jesus. She asked Jesus what to do with the oil; he told her to use it for anointing people with whom she prays, so she does that.

In the spring of 1992, Jesus told Annie not to take on any more projects until she completes two books. The first, *Inner Healing through the Rosary*, was published in the fall of 1992.

She began the first book in this way. On Monday, March 23, 1992, Annie went to confession. The confession went on for some time, and Annie received a new awareness of many things in her life, and tears. When she got home, she showered, then sat on the edge of the bed and pulled a T-shirt from a pile of clean but as yet not folded laundry on her bed and put it on. Immediately she felt a strong presence and a great warmth in her ears and head and hands and feet. She got out a notebook and a pen and began to write furiously.

Eric went to sleep, but Annie wrote until two the next morning.

She had begun her first book. The Lord had given her the title and the plan of the book, and helped her begin it. When, just before going to bed in the early morning hours, Annie looked at the T-shirt she was wearing, she saw that on the front was an image of our Lady holding a rosary in one hand and a scapular in the other. Above the image are the words, "Pray the rosary," and below the image it reads, "for peace".

Annie's second book takes up the subject of daily examination of conscience. In writing this second book, she frequently refers to the Bible. Jesus has her read a passage and then tells her what verse to use. Or He will just tell her to open the Bible at random, and then He shows her the verse or verses to go into the book.

Eric fully supports everything that Annie does and helps her. After graduating from Loyola Marymount College in Los Angeles with a bachelor's degree in business administration, Eric completed the necessary courses and student teaching at Ottawa University, a small college in Phoenix, to qualify as an elementary school teacher in Arizona. However, open to whatever way the Lord leads Annie and him, he is at present ministering full-time with Annie. When Annie prays over people, Eric prays with her.

- V -
Witnesses

One of the most encouraging fruits of the special presence of Jesus and His Mother at Scottsdale is the number of young adults who have moved into the parish. Sometimes successful and prosperous, sometimes with personal difficulties or professional worries, these young men and women are finding the only true and satisfying life - they have heard of this parish, of its life centered on and radiating from the Eucharist, and of its prayer group for young adults. They came to see, and they are moving in.

One young woman writes:

"How my life has changed since my conversion started at Saint Maria Goretti in 1988! Five years ago I was in the category of 'yuppie'. My life revolved around my work and studying for the exams required for the job. The rest of the time I was watching television, and going to 'happy hours'. I did not have specific goals, but I was successful in my career and earned a more-than-comfortable income.

"For all practical purposes I had left the Church soon after college. I was a 'cradle Catholic' who found parishes dry and lifeless. So I would 'try out' the new parish whenever I moved, which was pretty often. I would usually get bored, distracted, and frustrated, and would feel like a hypocrite for being there and not praying, so I wouldn't go back until my

'Catholic guilt' acted up again. Then I would return, and have another bad experience.

"My awareness of God completely deteriorated to the point where I just had a vague awareness that there was a God out there ... somewhere.

"This 'trying out' of churches went on from 1980 until early 1988 when I 'happened' to move into Saint Maria Goretti Parish. I 'tried out' the Teen and Young Adult Masses and still remember vividly two of my reactions: 'People really pray here!' and 'This is home!' So I started attending Mass regularly.

"But that was only the beginning. I. remember hearing about our Lady appearing in Medjugorje, Yugoslavia, and thinking, 'Oh that's nice.' I believed it on some level, but it did not call me on.

"I began participating in the young adults' prayer group at Saint Maria Goretti's because it seemed like the 'cool' thing to do. I guess God was just prepping me up for the things to come, because at this point I was still doing everything on the surface (praying with my mouth and not with my heart), without realizing what was happening at our parish. I didn't know the meaning of conversion and opening one's heart.

"Then in November of 1988 our Lady spoke directly to the prayer group through Stefanie. As she spoke, I knew in the deepest part of me that it was our Lady. I had no doubt whatever. This was the most traumatic experience I have ever had in my life because it shook me to my roots. I had believed our Lady existed and was sweet and wonderful, but way out there, somewhere out of reach. I had believed that she appeared to people and got involved in their lives, but only thousands of miles away in Yugoslavia or France or Portugal, not here in this small group of young adults in Scottsdale, not in a group that I am part of!

"I spent the next three days alone, in bed, because I became physically ill from emotional turmoil as I tried to reconcile what I knew to be true with what I had believed was true. I thought I was a good Catholic Christian; but if God — the Father, Son and Holy Spirit — were so close to me and cared so much for me, I had seriously to evaluate and change my life. God suddenly became One who cannot be taken lightly and cannot be kept at a distance.

"So I went through some of the conversion process of being 'Gung-ho for Jesus'! - and praying and re-ordering my life.

"A few months later I started getting very dissatisfied with my work. It seemed so pointless in the picture of the Kingdom of God that I now had, and it took all of my mental and emotional energy, leaving nothing for God (the way I saw it). I wanted to do something I considered more worthwhile and concerned with eternity, but I didn't know what. I cut down my hours to part-time so I could pray more and figure out what to do next. But even that was not enough. I was working at a job which up until recently had been my god. I quit a few months later, to clear my head and to try to discover my calling, but no answers came. I went back to part-time work in another company. I didn't like it, but it paid the bills, and it seemed to be the place God wanted me to be.

"Finally, in 1991 I quit my job to return to school to pursue a Master's Degree in Theology and Christian Ministry at a Catholic university. I am not passing judgment on the work I was doing - I just did not belong there. The primary work of the lay people of the Church is working in the world, helping to sanctify it and manifesting Christ to others, not by leaving their jobs to work for the Church, but precisely by remaining and working in the world. (Christifideles Laici, e.g. pp.36-37)

"Outwardly, my life has changed dramatically: from successful business woman with her own home, to poor college student; from being comfortable financially, to being very uncomfortable financially; from being independent, to being dependent; from having my life planned out, to having very few concrete plans at all. And I would not go back. I can now watch for the return of my old depression and ask God for His aid in discovering and confronting its cause. I realize that I have spent most of my life trying to be the perfect daughter, the perfect business woman, the perfect friend. And since I was never the perfect anything, I was always unhappy.

"But the changes in my life that are most important and that I am most thankful for are the changes inside. I now have a reason for living - to love and serve God. No matter how imperfectly I live that goal, I have the security of knowing that God loves me and will forgive me; that this Supreme Being who can and will do more than we can ask or imagine, not only cares about the world in general, but also cares about me in my present, past and future, more than I even care about myself.

"If I could choose one word to characterize all the changes I have undergone in turning my life to God, it is 'freedom': freedom to love (both God and others) because I am loved; freedom to give because I have been and am being given to; freedom to live according to my own personality and spirituality, because God chose to make me this way. Christ came to free us from the bondage of sin and death, and I am tasting that freedom. My life isn't all peaches and cream now, but I do have new eyes to see, new ears to hear and a new mind to understand. And at the times when I don't see or understand, I can rely on faith - that God knows what He is doing and wants only the best for us, His children."

Another writes: "The feast of our guardian angels, October 2, 1992, coincided with the young adults' prayer group meeting. Jesus, in his message to the group, told us about our angels. He said: 'Look to the angels; they will guide you.' The things I have done in front of my angel! He was always there with me: in high school when I did not want to live any more; when I was so mad at Jesus for making my father sick; in college when I did everything I wasn't supposed to do. He was there at my side, watching me - crying. I made it through high school. I made it through college. All the while with my angel watching. And even though I committed horrible sins, he waited for me. How I must have made him sad, ignoring him.

"Then Jesus moved me to Arizona. I heard about Saint Maria Goretti and the special things that happen there, how it is supposed to be the center of Jesus's mercy, how apparitions are occurring. I read some of the lessons that Jesus gave here. I then heard about the young adults' prayer group. I came once and was impressed and felt very warm and intrigued at how many people my own age filtered into the dimly lit tabernacle and knelt before the glowing cross which had water running and flowing at the bottom of it. There was such reverence, and I didn't know why.

"At that time, school still came first, so I left; and I did not go back for a while. But I started going to church on Sundays, and for some reason I just began to feel happier. My desire to pray and to read more about what Jesus was saying increased. I began to want to pray.

"That Christmas I went home and gave holy (blessed) water as Christmas presents. I realized then that I wanted to live my life for Jesus. I've grown to love Him with all my heart. He tells us to trust Him; He tells us He loves us; He tells us He will protect us. The blessed Mother tells us to give our worries to Him, that He loves us so much, and she loves us. She asks us for prayer, penance and fasting. She tells us to go before her Son in silence.

"I quit my job because it was keeping me from Jesus. If I would only have known earlier what I know now! But Jesus showed me that He waits for us. He is so patient, and He will never turn us away. People who knew me back home like me more and say I'm happier. It is just that I have Jesus with me all the time. He is the one that makes me happy. The Holy Spirit makes me smile! The Father guides my life."

Some years ago in Medjugorje, Father Tomislav Vlasic remarked to us: "There are those in the parish who have benefited more from the apparitions than the visionaries themselves, because they have taken up this way of life (taught by our Lady) and have begun to live it." The witness of an older man in the parish of Saint Maria Goretti illustrates this. He looked uncomfortable when someone asked him how he came to be involved. "Well, to be honest," he admitted, "I bought a property near here because it was a few minutes from the stadium of my favorite baseball team." Looking ever more doubtful, he continued, "I was driving past and saw this church, so I got out of my car. The atmosphere! I asked someone 'Is this a monastery or something?' To tell you the truth, I haven't been to a single baseball game yet. Apart from putting on the television sometimes to check the scores - I haven't been to a game." He has taken up this "way", and it is his whole life, his happiness.

The messages given by Jesus and our Lady at Scottsdale are powerful. They took this young executive by surprise:

"I was always a lukewarm Catholic and really thought church was a waste of time. Therefore I would go only once in a while to Mass. When I did go it was out of custom and respect for my parents, especially my mom; my dad never really went to church that much. Truly, going to church and receiving the Eucharist was at the bottom of my list.

"I guess I was a normal teen-ager. I had a good time, messed around a lot, studied, got drunk on week-ends, had a sexual relationship with my girlfriend, and smoked some 'pot' every once in a while. 'No big deal.' I had two ambitions: one was to become an astronaut, and the second was to be a millionaire and have tons of horses.

"One good day when I was talking on the phone with my mother, she asked me to buy her some books. She told me the name of the books (My Jesus of Mercy) and the name of the place where I could purchase them (Saint Maria Goretti Church). She also added, 'By the way, there is a prayer group for young people there, and maybe you would like to go to it.' I said to her, 'We'll see.' But I said to myself, 'Forget it! I've never gone to a prayer group in my life.'

"Anyway, about a month later she asked me about the books. I had completely forgotten about them; I felt sort of bad. I told her some excuse that I had been too busy and that

I would go buy them this week. I picked up the yellow pages found Saint Maria Goretti and called the parish office. They gave me directions (the church was very far from where I was), and the following day I drove to the church. I went into the office, asked them for the books and was surprised how inexpensive they were. Immediately after I left the church, as I was hungry I went to a restaurant. I was by myself so decided to read the books while I ate. And from that day on, my life has never been the same again.

"Immediately I was very moved and absorbed by the lessons. I couldn't put the book down. The lessons seemed to be very logical, very straight forward, easy to read, and at the same time answered a lot of questions. I finished the first two volumes relatively quickly. But then I became very busy with my work and sort-of forgot about them. Every once in a while I would read some of the lessons before going to bed at night. Out of the blue, about three months later I decided to go to the prayer group for 'young people' that my mother had talked about earlier. Meanwhile I had begun to go every Sunday to a nearby church, and I also went to confession. I hadn't gone to confession in three to four years.

"I called Saint Maria Goretti's and asked about the prayer group. The following Friday I went by myself. I didn't know anyone, so I felt a little uncomfortable. When I arrived at the tabernacle chapel, I was surprised to see the exposed Eucharist in the middle of the room. I had never before prayed before the exposed Eucharist. I started looking round, not sure of what we were going to do. A little later Carol welcomed everyone, and we began to pray the Chaplet of Divine Mercy. I had never heard the chaplet before but thought it was the most beautiful prayer I had ever heard. Next we prayed the rosary. I didn't remember how to pray the rosary since I had only prayed it three or four times in my life before, and then only at funerals. During the prayer I felt a wonderful peace. We then had shared prayer, and then everyone went outside to socialize. I decided to approach some people and make friends, and then I went home.

"The following week I invited some friends that I knew were Catholics and that wouldn't think I was crazy. This time our Lord gave a message through Gianna. I immediately recognized the tone of the message as the same one in the books. I truly was in a state of shock; I did not expect this. I felt energy going through me, and I thought my head was going to explode. But then I felt very relaxed. I thought I was going to fall out of my chair. That night I drove back home very excited. I had no doubts in my mind that it was truly Jesus speaking to us. I was on a Holy Spirit high. The following Sunday I went to my local church, and it was a whole different experience. Maybe, for the first time in a long time I knew Jesus was there. I also felt sort of holy.

"After that my life changed quickly, but peacefully. Rarely do I not go to the prayer group. I stopped putting so much importance on my work. I stopped putting so much importance on becoming a rich and successful business man. I began to put more importance in praying, in going to holy Mass, in going to confession, in living the moment, in trying to better myself.

"After about a month of going to the prayer group. I broke up with my girlfriend with whom I had been having a sexual relationship. I stopped getting drunk practically every week-end, and I was also reading the "Jesus of Mercy" books every night, over and over. And I began to purchase other religious books.

"After two months of going to the prayer group I made a personal promise to our Lord and our Lady that I would pray either the rosary or the chaplet of divine mercy every day for the rest of my life. Wow! I couldn't believe it when I said that. Yet I realize now, this was a very important commitment I made, because since then my faith had grown in leaps and bounds.

"A few months later I met the youth minister of my own church and joined the core team for a new "teen" program he was starting. I began going to frequent confession, initially every week. But after a while I was having a difficult time knowing what to confess. I now go at least every three or four weeks. Then I began going to daily Mass. After a year I had the desire to become a priest. Things were moving so quickly that I felt the need to slow down. And so I continue to discern my possible vocation to the priesthood.

"Through all this I have learned to love Jesus, not only as our Lord and Creator, but also as a friend. The single most important thing I have learned since I began to pray every day is intimacy with our Lord. In the Friday night messages, our Lord and our Lady frequently stress that they are with us always and everywhere. They always remind us of how much they love us and how we have nothing, absolutely nothing, to fear. Today, I am trying to make my life a prayer, by praying from the moment I wake up in the morning to the moment I go to sleep at night. I invite Jesus to go to work with me, to go shopping with me, to spend the entire day with me. I have learned, slowly, to give control of my life to Jesus. I have learned about Jesus' infinite mercy; I have learned to sacrifice; I have learned how to genuinely <u>love</u>."

Here is another angle on the messages:

"Instead of telling what the messages have done for me, I want to first say what they haven't done for me. The messages haven't promised me an easy life, spiritually, emotionally or physically. The messages haven't demanded instant holiness from me nor magically produced it. They haven't eliminated all fear from my life completely. But the biggest thing the messages haven't done is the messages haven't deceived me. The messages are full of mercy, wisdom, purity, love and forgiveness. They are the reflection of the God we all desperately thirst for, but who we find so difficult to reach in our material world.

"In their messages and lessons, Jesus and Mary have explained to us simply and in a straight forward manner that they are as close to us as our own breath. I have learned of God's desire for His people's intimacy and love. For the first time in my life I have been given a valid reason why there is suffering in my life and in the world. The messages have given me a peace unmatched, one I would not be able to attain through any means except by coming closer to our Lord.

"The messages have taught me what our Lord loves and what He hates. He hates rivals in front of him. Previously my career, among other things, was His rival in my life. I know now, we must pray for the grace to remove whatever that rival may be.

"I have learned God's grace is a great and tangible thing. It is not just some spiritual term repeated hundreds of times in the holy Bible. The messages of Scottsdale from our Lord and our Lady have given me a great desire for holy Mass, the Eucharist and the sacrament of Reconciliation. The messages have introduced me to the power of prayer - to be the action of my prayer, but to rely on our Lord for <u>everything.</u>

"Finally, the messages have taught me to stop running from my cross. Instead, I'm trying to imitate our Lord and embrace it, placing it squarely on my shoulders and proceeding with faith, counting on my prayer and His mercy."

A young adult writes: "Eighteen months ago I could best have been described as a 'buffet-line' Catholic. Like most young Catholics I went through my faith picking the sacraments, commandments and Church guidance that fit my tastes. If I didn't like something, it was left behind.

"At this time I was working in the news department for a television station in a large city. Each day for four years I helped deliver the horrific images that have become commonplace across the 'land of the free and the home of the brave': stories of brutal violence, epidemics of drugs and disease, corruption, sexual abuse, and many murders both in and out of mothers' wombs. The images were relentless, and left me with little hope.

"In November of that year I visited Saint Maria Goretti parish in Scottsdale, after hearing of the reported apparitions and messages. I thought it would make a good news series;

after all, the market I was working for was in an area heavily Catholic. I went to the News Director and the General Manager of the station 'pitching' the series idea and explaining that many people from our city had made pilgrimages to Scottsdale. I showed them a tape of the 'Miracle of the Sun' captured on home-video by an elderly Scottsdale woman. I mentioned other stations' interest in the story and that a book about the events was almost finished and would soon be published. The manager was slow in coming, but ultimately the station decided against the idea. Later that week I learned the apparition series was dismissed to accommodate another series: 'Sexual Abuse in the Clergy'.

"I was disgusted with the distorted interests and lopsided coverage of my employer. I prayed the blessed Virgin would intercede and allow me to somehow quit my job. Shortly after my prayer, my boss informed me my pay was being cut by fifty-percent and to either take it or leave it. I left it and thanked the blessed Mother as I cleaned out my desk.

"What I found in Scottsdale, particularly among the young adults, was a sincere attraction for and deep appreciation of the sacraments, the Eucharist and holy Mass. I know the out pouring of reverence I witnessed could never be orchestrated by a human being. Not by my own worthiness, but by God's grace I was shown that faith was a gift. I saw that faith around me and I wanted it for myself. So I asked how I could have faith. 'Go and pray before the blessed Sacrament,' they said, 'and ask him with an open heart for His mercy, and He will answer you.'

"I've learned that faith is not a feeling or an emotion of a privileged few. Faith is fact. I learned that faith doesn't eliminate life's obstacles; it overcomes them. I also learned the three most important words in the human language: Pray, Pray, Pray."

Each witness touched by the message of Scottsdale has been captivated in their encounter with Jesus. They have been carried beyond the words of the messages to the living, beating Heart of the Person who is Jesus. The following well illustrates this:

"When asked to explain what the messages of our Lord and our Lady here at Scottsdale mean to me, I thought I would do well to return to the basics, to the core of what was responsible for the initial steps of my conversion.

"So I opened Volume I of the <u>I Am Your Jesus Of Mercy</u> books, and there it was: In the very first message of the entire book - the answer I was looking for:

September 20, 1988, from our Lord –

'My child, I would like you to start being and living the holiness of me. ...'

It seems so long ago since I first read that. It has only been about ten months, but it seems long ago, probably because I have walked so far with our Lord since then. (And I still have so much further to walk.)

The message continues:

'... not only in your actions, but in your daily thoughts and feelings. Do not be holy on the surface, be holy within and throughout your entire body. BE ME!'

Did you get that last part? <u>BE</u> <u>ME</u>!

"That is the message. The call. The challenge. And it is the least we can do in return for all He has done for us. BE HIM! At least, <u>try</u>.

"It is our personal invitation to join Jesus in eternal life, an invitation given by the author of life himself. All we have to do is say 'yes'. And keep saying yes every day, every minute, with every thought He brings us. If we say 'yes' and open our hearts to our Lord and our Lady, they will do the rest.

"Pretty simple really. Not easy. Actually it is a difficult challenge but a simple process, and our Lord and our Lady will hold our hands and lead us every step of the way.

"Like many of us I was once a very, very lost sheep. But because of mercy and love I cannot possibly comprehend, our heavenly Father has brought me back to His flock. Through His grace He allowed our Lady to reach out and turn me back to her Jesus. They gave me the strength to say 'yes', taught me the importance of prayer, and changed my life for all eternity.

"A simple process. A challenging call. A heavenly reward."

Jesus can turn around the most hopeless of lives - if we give Him the chance.

"I have just been reading Matthew 23:25 where Jesus says,

'Woe to you ... hypocrites!

'You clean the outside of the cup and the dish, but inside they are full of greed and self-indulgence. Blind! ... First clean the inside, then the outside will also be clean.

"That was what my life was like until I found that this IS a time for our Lord's mercy!! The time is NOW!! I was making sure the outside looked great for everyone to see. Cleaning the inside of my life has been tough! So much had happened to me, but so much good has come out of it, and it was only because Jesus and Mary helped me to clean the inside of my cup and continue to help me every day.

"I was a very lost little girl. Not feeling much emotional support or love from my family caused me to seek it in my friends. I was born and raised in a strict Catholic family, and I went along with everything 'just-because-that-is-what-you-are-supposed-to-do-don't-ask-any-questions'!

"I rebelled incredibly at the age of sixteen. I started drinking a lot and smoking pot occasionally. Little did I know how much I was going to mess up. I became very bitter and angry with my family. I was known as 'the problem child'. It almost seemed useless to try to change. I began to date. By eighteen I lost my virginity, still trying to feel love which I thought meant intimacy which I thought meant sex.

"I searched for this intimacy for nine more years, coming up empty and more lonely each time. Through these years I had three abortions which piled up more self hate and no sense of self worth. I started drinking more heavily, doing harder drugs, getting very materialistic, trying to hide all the pain. I remember thinking to myself, 'I'm finally going somewhere!' I hit rock bottom; that's where I went!! I went into a deep depression. At the time I was dating someone;

and when he broke up with me, his last words were 'You need help'.

"That was when Jesus picked me up off the concrete. I had heard about our Lady appearing - it fascinated me that the blessed Mother could <u>possibly</u> be appearing in our age. I wanted to go there, but I was broke. Just then my aunt happened to be organizing a group. My parents called me up and offered to pay my way. It was a tour, visiting various cities, so our time in the parish was so short. But when Jesus and Mary are serious, they work fast!!!!

"I knew in my heart that I had to go to confession. But it wasn't until we were almost leaving that I was able to get to a priest. He said, 'It must be God's will that you see me.' I told him about my abortions ... I think I confessed this probably eight to ten times, but never felt truly forgiven. I started to cry hysterically. I remember the priest saying it's not only the abortion as being the sin; that was the result of the sin. The sin is how many times you have abused your body and your sexuality. I remember him saying 'Now honey, let's think back.' Just something, you know Jesus would say! He took me through seven years of abusive relationships. It was so painful, yet so freeing!! I'll <u>never</u> forget it. It was truly Jesus holding my hand through the whole thing! He was so gentle, so non-judgmental.

"The last thing to do was to name my children because yes, they **are truly my children**!!! I named them Kathryn, John and Mary. When he absolved me from my sins I saw darkness leave me and a bright light come in. Wow!!! The **mercy** of my Lord!!!! I went over to the other side of the church still sobbing. When I sat down, I heard three distinct voices say to me, "We love you Mommy"! Oh my gosh, I really **am** a mom!!! I really do have my children back. I can't see them, but they can see me! They love me!!! After what I did, they still love me!!!!! I can choose to love them back or reject them. I chose to love my little ones and feel the happiness and peace they bring me.

"This was four years ago. These last four years have seen a lot of growing pains, but also the most peace and love I have ever felt in my entire life! Jesus is <u>still</u> healing me of all my sinfulness and will continue to do so until the day I die. I thank Him and our beautiful Mother for giving me the chance to turn my life around!! For helping me to clean the inside of my cup little by little and helping me to become the beautiful woman that He created me to be from the very beginning!! Thank you my Jesus and my Mother Mary for helping me to love myself more and more each day!!! I LOVE YOU SO MUCH!!!!

- VII -
What Does Scottsdale Mean?

How can we evaluate the authenticity of the events taking place in Scottsdale, and of the messages that persons there receive? And how can we interpret the events and the messages? What meaning does Scottsdale have for us today? The questions have importance because many of the messages, all of those reported in this book, and the whole fact of the Scottsdale apparitions and locutions have as their intended audience not only the persons to whom Jesus or Mary apparently speak, but all of us, the world.

Theology traditionally distinguishes between "public revelation" and "private revelation". Public revelation is that contained in Scripture, in the Old and the New Testaments. Public revelation has ended, finished with the death of the last apostle. Private revelation, on the other hand, describes visions, apparitions, and words given to individual persons, for their own spiritual lives, for their own good, since the close of public revelation. But what about revelation that comes after the earliest times of Christianity and that purports to address itself not to individuals or to a particular group, but to all Christians or to the world? Certainly it cannot place itself at the level of the Bible. And yet, if authentic, it comes from God and has the character of divinely inspired communication. It falls somewhere between public and private revelation. Perhaps we can call it semi-public revelation.

What do we do with it? Should we believe everything that claims to come from God? Can we believe anything that claims to come from God but that comes after the formation of the Bible?

Should we believe everything that claims divine origin? Certainly not. If we did, we would accept every visionary in our time that reportedly sees and speaks with Jesus or with His Mother or with both. And there are hundreds today all over the world. The Sacred Congregation for the Doctrine of the Faith receives reports weekly, or more often, of claimed apparitions or locutions. And those are only the Catholics and only the ones that the bishops send to Rome.

"New Age" phenomena proliferate and include: mediums, pretended prophecy and prediction of the future, and channeling through people on earth from entities allegedly from elsewhere [heaven, hell, other planets]. Has there ever been an age of more prevalent false mysticism? And so, too, we hear about many revelations of Jesus and Mary, surely not all of them real.

We live in a time when, it seems, God goes to great lengths to get our attention, a time when Jesus and Mary do seem to communicate to many people in many parts of the globe. In such a time, we can expect many, many more false apparitions than true, many more unauthentic revelations than authentic. We can expect lots of "copy-cat" apparitions and locutions. To which, if any, do we give credibility? To which *should* we give credibility? And, another question, to which ones *can* we give credibility? What should I believe? What can I believe?

What can I believe? Whether Catholic or Protestant or non-Christian, I remain free to believe what I want to believe over and above the accepted revelation essential to my faith. A Roman Catholic, for example, holds all that the Church teaches, including of course the entire Bible, but stays free to believe more. That includes belief in private revelation or in what we have referred to as "semi-public" revelation. The Catholic Church has not approved the apparitions of our Lady at Medjugorje in Bosnia-Herzegovina, but millions of Catholics legitimately believe in them already.

How then can I evaluate the events at Scottsdale? I can believe in it. But should I? Is it true? What evidence do I have? What criteria can I use?

One way is to apply the criteria that the Catholic Church uses in arriving at least at a tentative conclusion regarding reported apparitions and locutions. Here they are.

1. Are the facts as they are reported to be, at least with a high degree of probability?

2. Are the people involved, those who receive the alleged apparitions and messages, sound psychologically and morally; are they sincere and honest, and do they respect Church authority? Is the situation free from evidence of collective hysteria or similar manifestations?

3. Are the messages attributed to Jesus or to Mary free from doctrinal error?

4. Do the events in fact promote a spirit of prayer, conversions of heart, and healthy religious devotion?

5. Does money making have little or no part to play?

If the answers to all of these questions are "yes" then, according to the standard directives from the Vatican's Sacred Congregation for the Doctrine of the Faith to the local investigating bishop, the bishop can at least provisorily hold the apparitions and the messages authentic.

What about Scottsdale? We have answered the above questions, to our own satisfaction, clearly in the affirmative. Our personal and private judgment [certainly we do not and cannot speak for the Church, but only as believing Christians] is quite positive.

After an at least tentative positive evaluation, the problem remains: what does all this mean? How can we interpret not only the messages, but also the whole situation, the entire complex of persons, apparitions, locutions and messages? What does it mean for us personally, for me and for you? How interpret the events and the messages, the whole message, of Scottsdale?

For one thing, our interpretation has to be in terms of the form that the events, including the messages, take. The Scottsdale events, in form, belong to a long-standing Judeo-Christian tradition of prophetic and apocalyptic divine manifestations, and we want to interpret them accordingly, according to that tradition.

The messages that come to us through Gianna and Stefanie have a strong prophetic style and content. The very language has a prophetic tone. These messages are prophecies.

Prophetic messages, prophecies, do not necessarily predict the future or even speak about the future. Sometimes they do, but often they do not. Prophecy calls us to repentance, or consoles us, or speaks to us about God and about our relationship with Him.

Prophecy can denounce immorality and injustice. It can announce the good news of Jesus, of God's mercy, of our salvation in Christ. Prophecy can direct us, guide us, or tell us what the future holds for us. The Scottsdale messages do what prophecy does. In particular, they call us to repentance; they speak to us of the Lord's mercy; they denounce immorality; they teach us about our relationship with the Lord. Most of all, they call us to conversion: to repent, to turn to the Lord, to accept His merciful love.

The messages are prophetic. Their context is apocalyptic. The events at Scottsdale have a clearly apocalyptic character. Prophecy tells what to do, calls us. Apocalyptic lets us know that God is doing something and that He intends to do more.

The fact itself of Scottsdale, that Mary appears there, that Mary and Jesus speak to certain people there, is apocalyptic. Apocalyptic understands history as under the lordship of Jesus, and it sees the future as totally submitted to God. Jesus is the Lord of history and of the future. He holds the future in His hands, hidden from us, and makes it present to us now in mysterious ways, in symbols and signs. And apocalyptic confronts evil squarely. Its clear vision of the power and the lordship of God enable it to see evil in all its terribleness. Our belief in the reality of Satan, in fact, comes from the apocalyptic tradition.

In the New Testament, the apocalyptic victory is already present in Jesus. He overcomes all evil - sin, death, the devil - by his own death and resurrection. The gospels show us the victory of Jesus not only in resurrection, but also in the healings and exorcisms that He does in His public ministry.

We can see apocalyptic elements in the Scottsdale events: especially in the facts of the apparitions and the messages, in the secrets that the Lord has given to some people, and in the healings that have taken place there.

The very fact of Scottsdale, that our Lady appears there, that Jesus speaks clearly to people there, is apocalyptic. It shows God breaking through from the ultimate future into our time, showing the power of His love in mysterious but unmistakable ways. The messages contain apocalyptic passages. For example, Jesus to Stefanie, "Soon you shall be called to answer for the arrogance of this world; the arrogance that defies my Father, misuses His gifts, and abuses His creations." And again, "I tell you the day shall soon come when you shall lose these possessions and the poor shall counsel you, but not with appearance, attitude, or advertising. With love they shall counsel you and have pity on you." The words, "soon you shall be called to answer," and, "the day shall soon come," are apocalyptic; they refer to the Lord's future actions of judgment.

And the secrets belong to the apocalyptic tradition. The Lord has given to some of the nine young people of Scottsdale secrets about the future. Gianna, Annie, and Susan, for example, have received secrets to be shared with others only at a certain time and under strictly specific conditions. These secrets for the most part regard serious and even catastrophic things that will happen to the world or to the Church in the near future.

Gianna has received secrets about woes that will come to the Church and to the world. The Lord has shown Annie admonishments and chastisements that await the world. Jesus has shown Susan, since her childhood, coming chastisements for the world. They frighten her for those who do not believe, or who, believing, do not return to God.

Secrets about the future classically mark apocalyptic situations. We do not know what the secrets say, only that they refer to grave future events. Secrets convey to us that although we do not know the future, the Lord does, and that He controls it entirely.

The reported healings at Scottsdale, most of them undocumented and unverified, let us know that the Lord acts there, that He is there in a special way, in power. And the fact that all these things go on tells us of the power and the presence of the Lord breaking into our history, this time in Scottsdale, Arizona.

What does all this mean for each one of us, for you and for me? For one thing, Mary is my mother in the spiritual order, a real mother who loves me and who cares enough about me to do and to say extraordinary things, this time in Scottsdale, to get my attention and to help me. She wants me to be sorry for my sins, to be converted, and to turn and to turn more to Jesus.

Scottsdale means that Jesus loves me, and that He calls me to turn to Him in conversion, to receive and to receive more His mercy and His love. Because I am spiritually blind, He draws a big and startling picture in Scottsdale; because I am spiritually deaf, He shouts at me through what He does in Scottsdale.

And Scottsdale means that, yes, we are in trouble. Would God go to such lengths if we were not in serious difficulty?

We do not know the nature of difficulties and trials coming soon for the Church and for the world. But we can be sure that they are coming. The point is not at all that we should fear what the future holds, but that we should be more converted and turn more to Him who holds the future, in trust and in confidence. He is lord, the lord of the future as well as of the present. We trust in Him.

- VIII -
Visiting Scottsdale

Thursday, October 1, 1992. The church of Saint Maria Goretti was filling up for the evening Mass. The day had been hot, even in early October. Outside the warmth lingered; but inside, the air conditioning cooled the church. I knelt at the back, a good position to observe. At the front of the church, three of the young women caught up in the Scottsdale events were kneeling in the first pew. Mary and Susan were there. Gianna had slipped in at the last moment. Father John Coleman, associate pastor, knelt beside them. Some of the young women's parents sat in the pew behind.

Usually the Thursday prayer meeting begins with the five joyful mysteries of the rosary, and then continues with the chaplet of Divine Mercy, a meditation on the passion of Jesus, which originated with the saintly Sister Faustina of Poland. Mass follows, and then the congregation recites the glorious mysteries of the rosary. The entire service lasts about two hours and a quarter. If our Lady does appear, she comes during the joyful mysteries of the rosary.

This evening the church was not quite full. I was told this was unusual. People of all ages were there. There were several young families with small children. A group of Indians knelt at the back near me. Here and there I could see people in wheel chairs.

The lighting was dim in the main church; two spot lights focussed on the sanctuary. This made details difficult to distinguish and was rather dazzling. No one who did not know what to expect would have observed the moment when our Lady appeared to Gianna. There was nothing to see, except that Gianna who had been half kneeling, half sitting, was now kneeling upright, her face turned in the direction of the statue of our Lady to the left in the sanctuary. Probably only those kneeling near saw the sudden movement, as though an electric shock had passed through her. There was no reaction in the congregation, no change at all. After eight minutes Gianna relaxed. Our Lady had left.

Mass began when the rosaries ended. More people arrived, including young people coming from work or school. Obviously their priority was the Mass, not the apparitions. One of the signs of the genuineness of the Scottsdale events is the lack of fanaticism. There is no hysteria. People do not come to <u>see</u> anything, because there is little to see. This is largely due to the balance achieved by the pastor Father Jack Spaulding and by the absence of personal vanity in the six young women and three young men. Now, before the Mass, Father Jack read, without comment and without indicating the authorship, the message which had been given to Gianna during those few minutes of the apparition, and which she had written immediately afterwards. This was the message, and it seemed clearly from the blessed Mother:

> My dear children, do not be upset or worried from the humiliation which comes from this present world. Shelter in our God and enjoy Him who lives in you. You can benefit from your weaknesses and fail-

ures, fears and doubts, by drawing good from your infirmities. My Son wishes to be your only nourishment and desire. God is your only support and only means of achieving holiness. Thank you, my dear little ones, for responding to my call. Peace to you. A blessing from my Son is upon you.

Father Jack celebrated Mass. After the deacon had read the gospel, Father Jack walked to the center front of the sanctuary. Speaking slowly, he gave this message, again without saying from whom it came. We could judge from the context that the message came from Jesus.

My dear ones, I invite you this night to come to me as children of my Father. I ask you again this night to trust in His will for you as I trusted, as my Mother trusted. This trust will assist you in living as the children of God. I am here with you to remind you of the love my Father has for you. He sent me once, and now He sends me again. I am with you. I tell you I love you also. Dear children of my Father, I bless you with my peace and with my mercy.

The Mass continued. At the end some people left, and others remained for the final rosary. This was an ordinary parish Mass, except that this was a week-day, the church had been full, and adoration of our Lord in the Eucharist continued in the Tabernacle chapel, as it does in this parish, twenty four hours, day and night.

Friday evening's meeting of the young adults' prayer group was atmospherically more impressive. About seventy young men and women met at 7.30 before the Tabernacle, in an hexagonal chapel with a central fountain. In the fountain stands a cross of open metal work, representing wheat and grapes. Four statues of angels look up in adoration, because at the conjunction of the two beams of the cross is a chalice shaped glass bowl containing the sacred hosts.

The chapel was in darkness except for the golden glow illuminating the cross and the four red lamps held by the angel figures. The chaplet of divine mercy, and the sorrowful mysteries of the rosary were recited slowly, meditatively. Usually either our Lord or our Lady gives a message through Mary or Stefanie or Gianna. On this evening, speaking quietly, Mary Cook spoke the message as it came to her.

A silence followed, and then came the intercessions. Spontaneously, the young people prayed for those who were in their hearts and for their own needs. Then Gianna spoke giving the message from Our Lord.

The meeting ended. Outside, groups met, discussing their week, making plans, going off to eat together - a Friday evening, with the week-end to anticipate. These are normal young adults, but they know one truth vital for their lives, an uncompromising truth, but to them the source of happiness - that we cannot be ambivalent towards Jesus our Lord.

HE WHO IS NOT WITH ME
IS AGAINST ME,
AND HE WHO DOES NOT
GATHER WITH ME, SCATTERS.

(Matthew 12:30)